Using

Quick Start to W

The WSGopher Window

Fetch button   Cancel or Stop buttons

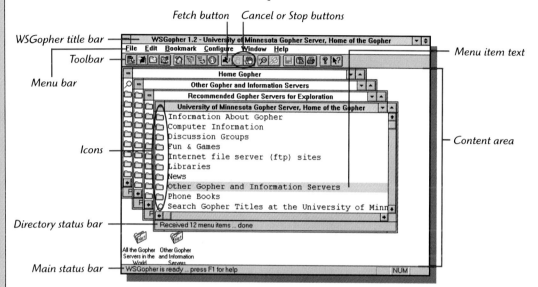

WSGopher title bar

Toolbar

Menu bar

Icons

Directory status bar

Main status bar

Menu item text

Content area

WSGopher title bar
This bar displays the name of the current Gopher directory and the version of WSGopher you're using.

Menu bar
The menus list all the commands and options of WSGopher.

Toolbar
The toolbar provides easy access to some commands.

Fetch button
Tell WSGopher to fetch the selected item with this button.

Cancel or stop buttons
Stop single or multiple WSGopher retrievals with these two buttons.

Content area
This area shows all the open Gopher directories, including directories minimized as icons along the bottom.

Menu item text
The text that follows the icons describes each Gopher item.

Icons
These icons tell you what kind of item this is (directory, text file, image file, and so on).

Directory status bar
The status bar for each directory tells you how many items there are in that directory, and if WSGopher is still retrieving them, or is done.

Main status bar
This bar tells you about menu items or toolbar buttons you select.

201 W. 103rd Street • Indianapolis, IN 46290 • (317) 581-3500
Copyright© 1995 Que Corporation

Searching with Gopher

If you want to find ...	Use this search tool
Items and menus on one particular Gopher server	Jughead search on that same Gopher server
Items and menus on all Gopher servers in the world	Veronica search
Files and documents on anonymous FTP sites throughout the world	Archie search
Text documents on a particular subject	WAIS database search

Searching with Jughead

- ■ Search for any word or combination of words
- ■ Use an asterisk (*) after a word or substring as a wild card
- ■ Use AND, OR, and NOT with combinations of words

This Jughead command	Does this
?help	Tells Jughead to show you its online help file
?version	Let's you find out what Jughead version you are using
?all	Returns all possible matched menu items
?limit=#	Limits the number of matched items to a designated number (#)
?range=#-#	Only returns a range of the matched search items

Searching with Veronica

- ■ Search for any word or combination of words
- ■ Use an asterisk (*) after a word or substring as a wild card
- ■ Use AND, OR, NOT, and parentheses ( ) with combinations of words

This Veronica command	Does this
-m#	Tells Veronica to find as many items as the number that follows it
-tcodes	Tells Veronica to only look for certain item types (when followed by one or more codes representing different Gopher item types)

Searching with Archie

Search for a word, a substring, or a regular expression

This Archie command	Does this
-e word	Searches for the occurrence of an exact word in the names of anonymous FTP files or directories
-s string	Searches for the occurrence of a string within the names of anonymous FTP files or directories
-r expression	Searches for matches to an Archie regular expression within the names of anonymous FTP files or directories

Searching with WAIS

Search for one or more words that appear in a collection of online text documents

Hot Gopher Sites

If you're looking for info on ...	Check out this site
Games	wuarchive.wustl.ed wiretap.spies.com pentagon.io.com gopher.tc.umn.edu
Recipes	ashpool.micro.umn.edu gopher.amhrt.org
Jokes and stuff	prism.nmt.edu dragon.camosun.bc.ca
Internet tools	gopher.tc.umn.edu gopher.mcmaster.c riceinfo.rice.edu
Utilities	cica-gopher.cica.indiana.edu gopher.archive.merit.edu micros.hensa.ac.uk cwis.usc.ed
Graphics	gopher.exploratorium.edu nmaa-ryder.si.edu libra.arch.umich.edu ucmp1.berkeley.edu
Sound files	hos.com gdead.berkeley.edu
Videos	wiretap.spies.com sunsite.unc.edu
Online books	gopher.etext.org world.std.com gopher.enews.com gopher.well.sf.ca.us
Government information	eryx.syr.edu gopher.counterpoint.com marvel.loc.gov gopher.house.gov gopher.senate.gov gopher.undp.org
UseNet news archives	watserv2.uwaterloo.ca jupiter.sun.csd.unb.ca
Weather maps	wx.atmos.uiuc.edu
Job postings	wcni.cis.umn.edu dartcms1.dartmouth.edu chronicle.merit.edu marathon.mit.edu acad-phy-sci.com
For sale/want to buy	people.human.com gopher.metronet.com
Sample hobby sites	culine.colorado.edu cycling.org leviathan.tamu.edu gopher.cs.tamu.edu

The WSGopher Toolbar

The buttons and what they do

Button	Function	Button	Function
	Opens the Fetch Bookmark dialog box		Cancels the most current WSGopher action
	Saves the selected item as a bookmark		Cancels all WSGopher actions
	Saves the entire directory as a bookmark		Finds text in a Gopher directory window
	Opens the Bookmark Editor		Finds the next occurrence of text
	Connects to your Home Gopher		Saves the current item
	Goes to the top level of the current Gopher		Copies the current item
	Goes up one level in the current Gopher		Prints the current item
	Opens the Item Information window		Shows information about WSGopher
	Fetches the selected Gopher item		Activates WSGopher's context-sensitive Help

Using

Gopher

PLUG YOURSELF INTO...

THE MACMILLAN INFORMATION SUPERLIBRARY™

Free information and vast computer resources from the world's leading computer book publisher—online!

FIND THE BOOKS THAT ARE RIGHT FOR YOU!

A complete online catalog, plus sample chapters and tables of contents give you an in-depth look at *all* of our books, including hard-to-find titles. It's the best way to find the books you need!

● STAY INFORMED with the latest computer industry news through our online newsletter, press releases, and customized Information SuperLibrary Reports.

● GET FAST ANSWERS to your questions about MCP books and software.

● VISIT our online bookstore for the latest information and editions!

● COMMUNICATE with our expert authors through e-mail and conferences.

● DOWNLOAD SOFTWARE from the immense MCP library:
    - Source code and files from MCP books
    - The best shareware, freeware, and demos

● DISCOVER HOT SPOTS on other parts of the Internet.

● WIN BOOKS in ongoing contests and giveaways!

TO PLUG INTO MCP: ➔ WORLD WIDE WEB: **http://www.mcp.com**

GOPHER: gopher.mcp.com

FTP: ftp.mcp.com

Using

Gopher

Keith Johnson

with

Philip Baczewski

Melody Childs

Using Gopher

Library of Congress Catalog No.: 95-67124

ISBN: 0-7897-0136-7

97 96 95   6 5 4 3 2 1

Interpretation of the printing code: the rightmost double-digit number is the year of the book's printing; the rightmost single-digit number, the number of the book's printing. For example, a printing code of 95-1 shows that the first printing of the book occurred in 1995.

Publisher: *Roland Elgey*
Associate Publisher: *Stacy Hiquet*
Publishing Director: *Brad R. Koch*
Senior Series Editor: *Chris Nelson*
Director of Editorial Services: *Elizabeth Keaffaber*
Managing Editor: *Sandy Doell*
Director of Marketing: *Lynn E. Zingraf*

Credits

Technical Writer
Noel Estabrook

Publishing Manager
Brad R. Koch

Acquisitions Editor
Beverly M. Eppink

Product Director
Mark Cierzniak

Production Editor
Kelli M. Brooks

Editor
Lori L. Cates

Technical Editor
Don Doherty

Acquisitions Coordinator
Ruth Slates

Operations Coordinator
Patty Brooks

Editorial Assistant
Andrea Duvall

Book Designer
Ruth Harvey

Cover Designer
Dan Armstrong

Production Team
Stephen Adams
Amy Cornwell
Amy Gornik
Karen Gregor
Bob LaRoche
Clair Schweinler

Indexer
Carol Sheehan

Composed in *ITC Century, ITC Highlander,* and *MCPdigital* by Que Corporation.

Dedication

To Richard and Imogene, Jerry and Geri, and my sweet Alice.

About the Authors

Keith Johnson has been writing about and providing support for commercial Internet products since 1992. He wrote documentation and help systems for WinGopher, and provided customer support for that product. Several of his manuals, including the *WinGopher Guides*, won awards from the Chicago chapter of The Society for Technical Communication. He currently works for Spyglass as a Mosaic support specialist. Since concentrating on Internet products, he's also gotten married, traveled in Central America, and rehabbed an 85-year-old house. He spends as much of his offline time as possible in the North Woods and kayaking the Great Lakes.

Philip Baczewski is the assistant director of academic computing for the University of North Texas Computing Center. He is the author of many articles about using the Internet and has contributed to several books on the subject. When he is not helping people use computers or the Internet, Baczewski makes use of his Doctorate in music composition and writes pieces for orchestra, orchestral instruments, or even computers. Two works, one for solo flute and another for 20-piece flute choir, have been published by JP Publications. His orchestral pieces have been performed by professional orchestras in Fort Worth and San Francisco. He also researches how professional musicians hear and understand music. In his spare time Baczewski likes to play golf, but unless he gets some more spare time, he may never score lower than 80.

Melody Childs is a messaging specialist at Indiana University in Bloomington, Indiana. She has been in the computing field since 1981, working for both private industry and in the university as an applications developer, consultant, technical writer, trainer, and e-mail adminstrator. She can be reached on the Internet as **mchilds@indiana.edu.**

Acknowledgments

To Beverly Eppink, who signed me up for this project, and to Mark Cierzniak and Kelli Brooks, who helped me finish it—thanks for their help and encouragement throughout.

To Mark "Gopher" Gobat, who's WinGopher really introduced me to the Internet as well as Gopher in '93, which seems so long ago now....

To Dave Brooks for writing WSGopher.

And mostly to my wife Alice, who put up with me while I got this written, reviewed most of my drafts, generally kept things together in our life, and planned vacations.

-Keith

My contribution to this book was made easier by the help and understanding of a number of people (and one small dog).

Thanks very much to Joni for understanding why I've spent so much time closeted with the computer.

Thanks to Beverly, Mark, and Kelli at Que for their great suggestions and help in putting my part together.

And thanks to Percy for putting up with a few shorter walks and a little less play time (yes, that's the dog).

-Philip

Trademarks

All terms mentioned in this book that are known to be trademarks or service marks have been appropriately capitalized. Que cannot attest to the accuracy of this information. Use of a term in this book should not be regarded as affecting the validity of any trademark or service mark.

We'd Like to Hear from You!

As part of our continuing effort to produce books of the highest possible quality, Que would like to hear your comments. To stay competitive, we *really* want you, as a computer book reader and user, to let us know what you like or dislike most about this book or other Que products.

You can mail comments, ideas, or suggestions for improving future editions to the address below, or send us a fax at (317) 581-4663. For the online inclined, Macmillan Computer Publishing has a forum on CompuServe (type **GO QUEBOOKS** at any prompt) through which our staff and authors are available for questions and comments. The address of our Internet site is **http://www.mcp.com** (World Wide Web).

In addition to exploring our forum, please feel free to contact me personally to discuss your opinions of this book: on CompuServe, I'm at 76245,476, and on the Internet, I'm **mcierzniak@que.mcp.com**.

Thanks in advance—your comments will help us to continue publishing the best books available on computer topics in today's market.

Mark Cierzniak
Product Development Specialist
Que Corporation
201 W. 103rd Street
Indianapolis, Indiana 46290
USA

Contents at a Glance

{ Table of Contents }

What can I find on Gopher?

see page 15

Chapter 2: What Do I Need to Gopher?

Part II: Starting to Use Gopher

Chapter 3: Getting Started with WSGopher

*What's all this stuff
on the screen?
see page 46*

Chapter 4: Navigating Gopherspace

Chapter 5: Using Bookmarks to Save Your Place

Chapter 6: Getting By with a Little Help from Your Friends

Chapter 7: Other Gopher Activities

*Change
the look of
WSGopher*

see page 119

Part III: Finding What You Want with Gopher

Chapter 8: Searching with Jughead

*Finding
information
and resources
with Jughead*

see page 129

Chapter 9: Searching with Veronica

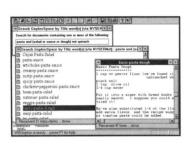

Chapter 10: Searching with Archie

*Using
Gopher
to retrieve
files from
anonymous
FTP sites*

see page 172

How is WAIS different from Veronica, Archie, and Jughead?

see page 176

Part IV: Burrowing into Everything

Chapter 12: Gophering from Online Services

Chapter 13: Gophering from the World Wide Web

How to spot a Gopher on the Web

see page 206

Part V: Finding Cool and Useful Gophers

Chapter 14: Listing of Gopher Sites

Need a job?
Use Gopher
to find one!

see page 238

Part VI: Gopher and Beyond

Chapter 15: The Future of Gopher

Part VII: Appendixes

Appendix A: Other Gopher Software

Appendix B: Understanding Internet Connections

"What kind of Internet connection can I get?"

see page 273

Part VIII: Indexes

Action Index

Index   285

Introduction

You've heard about everything that's out there on the Internet, maybe even seen some of it yourself. You've read about the Internet—it's hard not to these days. With all there is to learn, and all the newspapers, articles, magazines, and hype, how do you know where to start? How about a simple way to go and get things from the Internet?

How 'bout Gopher?

With an Internet connection in place, Gopher makes a daunting task a piece of cake. It shows you the Internet as lists to choose from. With Gopher, you can explore the Internet easily, and bring back all the files and information you find there—and entertainment, too (let's not take this Information Superhighway thing too seriously!).

There are lots of technical documents and files on the Internet about how Gopher works, and how to use it, but you don't have to read all of them. *Using Gopher* will get you started and teach you what you need to understand about Gopher. It will show you what to do with Gopher, and tell you where to look for what you want.

After you're up and running Gopher software, you'll find it easy to get around. Gopher lets you browse from computer to computer—no difficult commands to memorize, no need to know exactly where you're going. Gopher easily brings the resources of the Internet right to you

This book also introduces you to WSGopher, the most popular Gopher program for Windows. *Using Gopher* tells you where to get WSGopher (it's free on the Internet!), how to install it, and most importantly, how to use it to get the most out of Gopher and your Internet connection.

WSGopher makes it easy to point and click your way through the Internet. It helps you remember where things are so you can go back to something that interests you. It retrieves all types of files (sound, images, video, and text) and helps you play and display them.

This book will introduce you to Gopher, and Gopher will introduce you to the Internet. And the way things are going today, there's no telling where that might lead you.

What makes this book different?

The idea behind *Using Gopher* is to show you the strength of Gopher and the Internet. Because it focuses solely on Gopher (WSGopher in particular), it can provide useful details, as well as the overview you need to understand and use Gopher.

There are tips to help you use Gopher more efficiently and notes to give you useful pieces of information along the way. Cautions warn you about potential hazards, and Q&As answer your questions, hopefully before you ask. New terms are defined when they're introduced. It's all in plain English, without the buzzwords, hype, and techie talk.

If you're new to the Internet, this book will get you started and introduce you to Gopher. If you've used other parts of the Net, here you'll find all you need to know about Gopher.

How this book is put together

This is a book about Gopher in general, and WSGopher in particular. If you don't have WSGopher, *Using Gopher* will tell you how to download it for FREE from the Internet. If you don't use WSGopher, this book will help you better understand the Gopher software you do use.

 (Tip)

This book assumes you know the basics of the Internet, and that you have a connection. Because of the focus on Gopher, it doesn't provide in-depth instructions on getting you connected to the Internet. If you aren't yet connected, there are many books that will help you. Take a look at some of the other titles from Que, including Easy Internet and Using the Internet.

Part I: Getting to Know Gopher

For those who need to start at the beginning, here's an introduction to Gopher. It briefly tells you where Gopher came from, and what it can do for you. Most importantly, it tells you where to get a FREE copy of WSGopher, and how to install it.

Part II: Starting to Use Gopher

Now you're ready to delve into WSGopher, from launching the program the first time to using its powerful bookmarks and viewer features. You'll learn how to cruise Gopherspace, save your favorite places, retrieve files, and display them. We'll tell you how to save things you find with WSGopher, and how to tell WSGopher what to save and what to delete.

Part III: Finding What You Want with Gopher

Not finding what you want? You can search Gophers with tools like Veronica that searches everywhere, and Jughead that searches particular Gopher sites. We'll show you how to use these search tools and others to find specific information without wandering around lost in Gopherspace.

Part IV: Burrowing into Everything

Gophers turn up in the strangest places. You can gopher from major online services like AOL and CompuServe. We'll tell you how and show you what a Gopher looks like from there. It also tells you how to spot a Gopher in the World Wide Web, the newest part of the Internet.

Part V: Finding Cool and Useful Gophers

Get some starting points for your Gopher exploration. This list of Gophers and their addresses serves as a handy reference, no matter what Gopher software you use. Think of it as your Yellow Pages to Gopherspace.

Part VI: Gopher and Beyond

As the Internet continues to grow and evolve, what does the future hold for Gopher? Will it become obsolete? Chapter 15 discusses Gopher, its current limitations and its possibilities for tomorrow.

Part VII: Appendixes

Some assorted Gopher-related information. Here's an overview of other Windows Gopher programs—you may have used one of them. There's also a short description of Internet connections if you need the background information.

Part VIII: Indexes

To top it all off, this book includes an Action Index, in addition to the regular one, that is designed to track down the specific information you need when you need it.

Information that's easy to understand

This book uses a number of special elements and conventions to help you find information quickly—or skip stuff you don't want to read right now.

Information that you type to issue commands and Internet addresses that appear in the text are all in **bold type,** like this: **gopher.micro.umn.edu.** Messages and text that appear in the software are shown in a special typeface.

Throughout this book, we'll use a comma to separate the parts of a pull-down menu command. For example, to start a new document, you'll choose File, New. That means "Pull down the File menu, and choose New from the list."

And if you see two keys separated by a plus sign, such as Ctrl+X, that means to press and hold the first key, press the second key, and then release both keys.

(Tip)

Tips either point out easily overlooked information or help you use your software more efficiently, such as through a shortcut. Tips may help you solve or avoid problems.

<Caution>

Cautions warn you about potentially dangerous results. If you don't heed them, you could unknowingly do something harmful.

Q&A

What are Q&A notes?

Q&A notes appear as questions and answers. We try to anticipate user questions that might come up and provide answers here.

❝ ### Plain English, please!

These notes define—in plain English—technical terms or computer jargon when they appear for the first time. ❞

Sidebars are interesting nuggets of information

Sidebars include information that's relevant to the topic at hand, but not essential. You might want to read them when you're not online.

Here you may find more technical details, or interesting background information.

Part I:

Getting to Know Gopher

1
The Why, What, and Where of Gopher

If you need to find something on the Net but aren't sure where it is, or even exactly what you're looking for, let Gopher do the legwork.

In this chapter:

- Chaos on the Internet
- Bringing a little structure to the Net
- Where are all these Gophers?
- What can I find with Gopher?

We've all heard the stories about how the Internet started with relatively few people having access. Back in those days, you had to use command line software; there was no Windows software to make it easy. You had to FTP files yourself, and it was all uphill, both ways. Well, it goes something like that. The Internet grew, and people developed better tools, like Gopher, to help manage it.

Why do I need Gopher?

As the Internet grew, it contained more and more information, and more and more people had access to it. The information was spread across more computers and became harder and harder to keep track of. You had to know where something was before you could go get it.

You needed to know a computer's address to get to it. Every computer was organized in its own way, so you had to learn how to get around each one.

And you had to type in every command and address along the way. One misplaced character and you either went nowhere or botched a file retrieval and had to start over.

Picture each computer on the Internet as a library filled with books, connected to the other libraries. You might know your local library very well and be able to wander around it to find what you want. But what if your local library doesn't have the book you're looking for? Well, it's linked to all these other libraries. But how do you know where to start looking?

Gopher organizes things

All these other Internet libraries have useful information, but how can you know what's where? Each library has its own system, or no system at all, for its card catalog. Certain libraries have information only on very specific topics. How can you learn your way around a new library, even if you get lucky and connect to a new, useful site?

Enter Gopher, a way of organizing information on Internet computers and delivering that information to you. Gopher is like a standard card catalog to all the Internet libraries. Gopher gets you the books you need, regardless of where on the Internet they are.

Gopher organizes information into menus. The items on these menus are either other menus or files. When you select an item from a menu, Gopher displays it. This system of menus is very much the same, no matter what Gopher software product you use. It's kind of like ATM machines—they're all similar, no matter what bank they're with.

 Plain English, please!

Like menus in other computer systems and in more everyday occurrences, a Gopher **menu** is a list of choices. A Windows software menu lists commands like Open and Save, a diner's menu lists eggs and coffee, and a Gopher menu lists directories and files.

When you select an item from a Gopher menu, no matter where it is, Gopher brings it back to you. With Gopher, selecting something from a menu on a computer across the country becomes as easy as looking at a file on a machine at the local university. You select an item from a menu, and Gopher displays that item, wherever in the world it is.

Gopher cooperates with other parts of the Internet and with other software. This cooperation lets Gopher access even more of the Internet and many different kinds of files. Ultimately, your Gopher software can help you define what the Internet looks like to you.

A table of contents to the Internet

Let's continue the library example. Each computer on the Internet is like a library hooked to other libraries. Gopher presents a list of the things you find at one library, or computer, on the Internet. In some ways then, a Gopher menu is like the table of contents of an Internet computer. This comparison somewhat oversimplifies both Gopher and the Internet, but it's an easy way to understand the basics of how Gopher works.

A Gopher menu differs in one way from a typical table of contents in a book. When you turn to the Table of Contents in this book, for example, you see the entire table at once: Parts, Chapters, Main Headings, and Subheadings.

If we were to view the contents of this book with Gopher, the first "page" we see would look like this:

- Part I: Getting to Know Gopher

- Part II: Starting to Use Gopher

- Part III: Finding What You Want with Gopher

- Part IV: Burrowing into Everything

- Part V: Finding Cool and Useful Gophers

- Part VI: Gopher and Beyond

- Part VII: Appendixes

- Part VIII: Indexes

If we want to see what's included in Part I, we select it (probably by clicking our mouse on the screen text). Gopher then would go and get the things that are stored under Part I. It would bring back a list that looked like this:

- Chapter 1: The Why, What, and Where of Gopher

- Chapter 2: What Do I Need to Gopher?

If you select Chapter 1, perhaps Gopher would go and get the introductory text to this chapter, and the subheadings. You could then select the Subheading, "A table of contents to the Internet," and be able to read this very paragraph.

As you select items from a Gopher menu, you move from top-level information, like the Parts of this book, down to lower-level information, like the actual text of this chapter.

Figures 1.1 to 1.4 show examples of some Gopher menus from the University of Minnesota. Each figure moves further down the menus to more detailed information. The top level is the introductory menu to the University of Minnesota's Gopher site. The last level is a menu of Windows Gopher software applications that you can download from the University.

Fig. 1.1
A Gopher menu listing choices from a table of contents for this Gopher site.

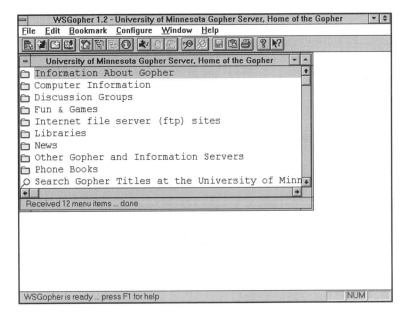

You'll notice that some items in these menus have different icons beside them than others. These icons represent the various kinds of Gopher items. Each Gopher software uses its own set of icons. In WSGopher, the software shown here, the file folders are directories that lead to menus of more Gopher items. See Chapter 3, "Getting Started with WSGopher," for a list of the other WSGopher icons.

Fig. 1.2
One level into the table of contents the information is slightly more specific. This menu has information about Gopher.

Fig. 1.3
Looking for Gopher software? You're getting warmer.

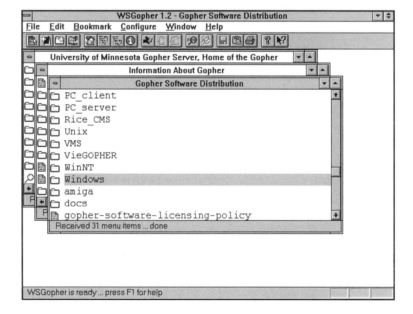

Fig. 1.4

Now you're there. At this level of the Gopher table of contents, there is content—Gopher software programs.

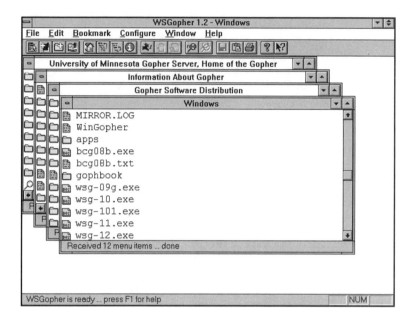

Each of the menus in this sample Gopher search contains a part of the table of contents of the Gopher site at the University of Minnesota. You can navigate much of this table of contents without leaving the University's Gopher site. You'll even connect to several different computers there.

However, some Gopher items at this site connect to computers at entirely different Gopher sites. That's the beauty of Gopher. Each table of contents can contain links to other tables of contents, which contain links to…and so on. As you explore further with Gopher, you'll see how these tables of contents are connected together across the Internet.

Gopher presents the Internet as a dynamic table of contents that points you to files instead of pages in a book. How that table of contents appears to you depends on what Gopher menu you are viewing. Because Gopher menus are linked, your view of the Internet changes and expands with every new computer Gopher takes you to.

So what's the top level of the Internet? In the real world, a table of contents has a top level—the Parts of this book, for example. But what's the *top* of the Internet? If you always start Gopher at the University of Minnesota, that becomes, in effect, the top level of the Internet for you. But if you start at some other Gopher site, then from your point of view, that site is the top level.

What can I find on Gopher?

Any of these types of Gopher sites and any site that doesn't fit easily into one of the categories listed in this section, can contain all kinds of things. Some sites are obvious locations for information on a particular subject. Some are master listings of all types of information.

As you'd expect, a Gopher site at the chemistry department of a major university has very different contents than a site at the United Nations. But don't be surprised if you find hidden treasures at any Gopher site, as well as links to unexpected places. It's hard to tell what's out there.

Here's a brief look at what you'll find in Gopherspace. This book will help you locate items by searching specifically for them, by browsing in likely places, or by just hunting around for them. For a detailed list of useful, interesting, and just cool Gopher sites, check out Chapter 14, "Listing of Gopher Sites."

Software

One of the great features of the Internet is that it lets people distribute their software without having the resources required for a full commercial product. If someone writes a useful program, like some of the Gopher software discussed in this book, he can let thousands of other people use it, by making it available on the Internet.

 **⊗<Caution>** Don't use Gopher, or anything else, to retrieve illegal copies of commercial software that is posted on the Net. Finding a free copy of an expensive program might seem too good to pass up, but legally, it could come back to haunt you.

Some sites are repositories for publicly available software. Some contain files more specific to that site. You'll find serious software that is useful for Net exploration as well as programs that are just for fun.

①(Tip)

Make sure you download files that are compatible to the system you are using. Obviously, you won't be able to successfully run Macintosh software if you're using a Windows machine. Gopher will go and get it for you though; that's its job.

Information

Information is a key buzzword on the Internet, and there's plenty of it in Gopherspace. From classic literature to online newspapers, from technical papers to daily weather forecasts, it's all out there.

Much of the information in Gopherspace is stored in text files. Gopher software retrieves those files for you, so that you can:

- Display and read the files

- Save them to your hard drive

- Cut and paste from them into other documents

Shareware—good software at great prices

Software programs you'll find in Gopherspace are usually shareware. **Shareware** is software that you're free to download and use before paying for. It's a "try before you buy" way to shop. If you like the product, the author asks that you pay a small fee for the license to keep using it.

Shareware is written by talented individuals who are willing to distribute their work via the Net, instead of through traditional commercial channels. Many of the programs are very good, and their authors deserve to be compensated for their work.

What do you get out of paying for your shareware? Shareware authors may provide updates, technical support, or documentation to the registered users of their applications. The information included with each program will tell you what to expect.

Lastly, registering and paying for the shareware you use makes you a legal licensee of the application. Licensing all the software you use means you avoid any potential legal problems involving unlicensed software.

Graphics, sound, and video

Other types of files found in Gopherspace are graphics, sound, and video files. Again, these files can be found in specific archives or scattered around at any site you encounter.

To play video or sound and to display graphics, Gopher hands the files off to other software. Software programs that Gopher uses for this are called viewers or helper applications. For more details, see Chapter 6, "Getting By with a Little Help from Your Friends."

What does Gopher do for me?

Gopher organizes things into menus. You select an item from a menu and Gopher goes and gets it. Basically, it is a simple way to organize the mass of information on the Internet. It provides a straightforward way to view information, combined with an easy way to retrieve that information.

Because of the way it organizes information, Gopher provides an easy way to get around the Internet. An item on a Gopher menu may connect to another directory or file on that same computer, or to a computer somewhere else on the Internet. The people who designed it describe Gopher as "burrowing" through the Internet.

People have set up Internet sites with Gopher in ways that allow you to burrow around the Net from computer to computer, without having to remember addresses or needing to know arcane commands. You can connect to places all over the Internet just by choosing items on a Gopher menu.

 (Tip)

How do you tell if a Gopher menu will connect you to a different computer? The description of the menu item often tells you what computer it's on. Most of the time, you don't need to know exactly where a menu will lead you. Gopher will take you there. Sometimes, however, you may notice that a Gopher item leads you to a site halfway around the world. Be prepared to wait, or find a similar item that's located closer to home.

You'll learn more about Gopher through exploring the Internet and through reading this book. There are sites with lots of links to computers all over the world. There are tools to help you find specific information, and ways to save Internet locations you want to visit again.

Understanding Gopher clients and servers

The Internet uses a type of computing called client-server. To put it simply, a **client** retrieves and displays information that is stored on a server. The **server** stores information until it's requested by a client. By splitting the workload, each piece of software can do what it does best.

The server half of the equation

For those of us accustomed to pointing and clicking, an Internet server is a fairly complicated bit of computing. Suffice it to say that the servers are where you access the files.

A Gopher server is software that stores files and waits for a client to request them. The server hardware is the actual computer that stores the information. Information on a Gopher server can be files that contain text, graphics, sound, video, software programs, and who knows what else.

How many servers fit on a server?

A single computer can run several different server software programs at the same time. Each server deals with information from different parts of the Internet.

The same computer that runs Gopher server software can also run software for the UseNet news FTP, or electronic mail Internet protocols.

How does the machine keep track? Although the machine itself has only one Internet address, it "listens" for incoming requests from each protocol on a different port. A server port is like the place on your PC where you plug in your modem. When a request comes in to a server, it goes to a specific port. The appropriate server software is listening for requests on that port.

The client half of the equation

Clients retrieve and display data. On the Internet, you use different types of clients for different kinds of data. You may already be familiar with some types of Internet clients.

If you've ever sent or received e-mail, then you've used an e-mail client. If you've read or posted UseNet news articles, then you've used a news client. To access files through Gopher, what kind of client would you use? A Gopher client, of course.

After a Gopher client connects to a server, it displays the files and directories stored on that server. Then, when you select a file for Gopher to retrieve, it opens a connection to get that file. It closes the connection when the retrieval is done.

The way Gopher works—opening and closing connections as needed—makes it more efficient. It only opens connections when it needs to, and only leaves the connection open while it retrieves the item.

Gopher and the rest of Internet

The team at the University of Minnesota that built Gopher designed a new way to burrow around the Net, but they didn't reinvent the wheel entirely. They took advantage of things already on the Internet. Gopher's simple menu interface is actually carrying out some very familiar Internet activities.

The Internet is a huge system of linked computers brimming with information. However, not all of that information is in the same part of the Internet. Different kinds of information are sent through different Internet protocols.

 Plain English, please!

Internet protocols are sets of rules that define how computers communicate. Think of them as a family of languages, like the Romance languages. These languages—Spanish, French, Italian, and Portuguese—are all based on Latin. They have similarities and differences, but they're related.

> The basic protocol, or language, of the Internet is **TCP/IP (Transmission Control Protocol/Internet Protocol)**. The other Internet protocols—FTP, UseNet, WWW, Telnet, Gopher, and others—are like the Romance languages that evolved from the Latin of the Internet protocols, TCP/IP. **"**

Gopher and FTP

A big part of what Gopher does is retrieve files. FTP is a great file retrieval protocol, so Gopher uses it to actually bring the file back across the Internet. Gopher FTPs so you don't have to.

Actually, many files that are now available through Gopher were originally available through FTP sites, and still may be. Because Gopher is so much easier to use, it made sense to put these files on Gopher computers, too.

To you, Gopher's use of FTP is invisible. Gopher lists the file on a menu, you select the file, Gopher performs an FTP retrieval, and bingo; the file is there for you to read, display, run, or save for later.

Gopher and Telnet

A Gopher menu can include files that contain information to start Telnet connections. When you select the Telnet item from the Gopher menu, Gopher retrieves the information about connecting. Then it launches a Telnet application and hands the connection information to that program. The Telnet program then actually makes the connection and you continue from there. Figure 1.5 shows a Telnet connection that's been launched from a Gopher program.

Probably the single largest set of Telnet links in Gopherspace are links to libraries. Many libraries have their computerized card catalogs available through Telnet. Gopher makes these catalogs easy to find and easy to connect to, but Telnet actually lets you search the catalog.

When you launch a Telnet session at a library, or anywhere else, you'll need to know how to complete the connection. Most sites provide a file with instructions that launch the Telnet connection. This instruction file tells you how to log in, what password to use, and other things you need to know. Remember, a Telnet session makes you a terminal on a remote computer. Each computer will have its own slightly different way of doing things.

The Rest of the Net—the short form

There are entire books that will introduce you to the Internet. Here's just a brief breakdown of the major parts of the Internet.

FTP (File Transfer Protocol)   Retrieves files from remote computers. FTP also lets you put a file on a remote computer. Tons of software on the Internet are available through FTP.

E-mail   Sends and receives electronic mail messages to anyone on the Internet, or even just on a network that has a gateway to the Internet. A great addition to business communication, and a good way to send a note to a long lost friend.

UseNet   The most diverse source of discussions, news, reference information, arcane knowledge, gossip, and sheer nonsense that you will ever encounter. UseNet newsgroups allow group discussions on specified topics. There are thousands and thousands of groups. You'll find one that interests you.

Telnet   Connects you to a computer and lets you log in as a terminal on that machine. With a Telnet connection you can run programs, check your e-mail, or read UseNet news. Many libraries make their card catalogs available via Telnet.

The World Wide Web Lets you navigate the Internet by simply clicking on a highlighted word or a graphic. From a Web page you can read text, view graphics, and even listen to sounds. It's sort of like several files rolled into one. The Web is the newest Internet protocol and incorporates information available through FTP, UseNet, and Gopher.

Gopher works with most of these protocols in some fashion. The only one that is excluded is e-mail. If you think about it, it makes sense. E-mail is usually for sending and receiving files one-to-one or between small groups. Gopher, on the other hand, is a way of delivering documents to many people.

Fig. 1.5
Gopher software helps launch a Telnet connection to the National University of Singapore's library.

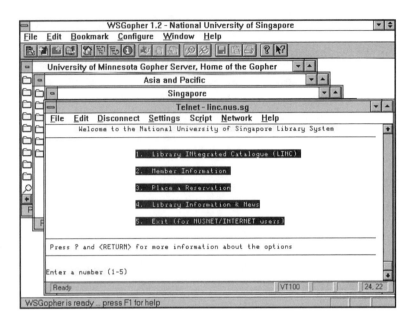

Gopher and news

Gopher can give you access to read live UseNet newsgroups. However, reading these messages is not the same as participating in the whole experience of UseNet news. There really is no substitution for an active Internet newsgroup. Figure 1.6 shows the articles from a newsgroup about Gopher.

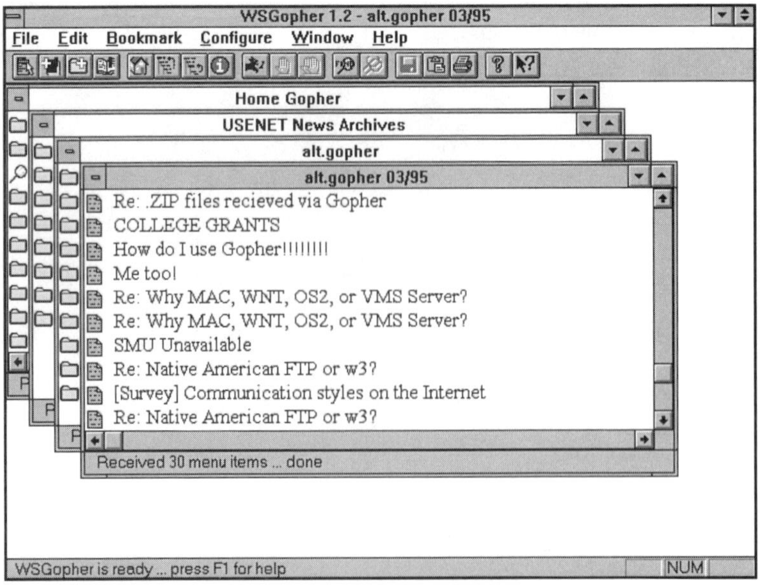

Fig. 1.6
Gopher software displays files from the newsgroup alt.gopher.

Some Gopher sites store UseNet files as news archives. These archives let you scan previously written articles and can be a useful source of information. Archives allow you to check out a group before you go online with UseNet.

❶ (Tip)

Many Gopher sites only allow registered users at that site to access UseNet. A university may only allow people within the school's system to get UseNet news through the Gopher there. There are publicly available news servers through Gopher, but it's better that you access it in other ways.

Your local access provider should either maintain a computer to access UseNet news or allow you to connect to one. With a full newsreader program and the access provider's news site, you'll get the full experience of UseNet.

It's not Gopher's fault that it doesn't fully access news. Gopher was never intended to be an all-in-one Internet solution. The various parts of the Internet require different tools, just like you need a different vehicle to travel through water than you do over land. Gopher provides you with a glimpse of UseNet, but to experience it fully, get a full-featured newsreader like WinVN. For a complete description of UseNet, get a copy of *Using UseNet Newsgroups*, also available from Que.

Gopher and the WWW

With Web software like Mosaic, you can access Gopher servers by entering a specific address, or simply by clicking highlighted text. Gopher directories display as a list of items on the Web page. You select any item by clicking on it. Figure 1.7 shows a Gopher directory displayed in Mosaic.

For more information on using Gopher with Web software, see Chapter 13, "Gophering from the World Wide Web."

Fig. 1.7
NCSA Mosaic 2.0.0b4, a popular Web browser, displays the Gopher directory from the University of Minnesota. Do you still recognize this Gopher site from figure 1.1?

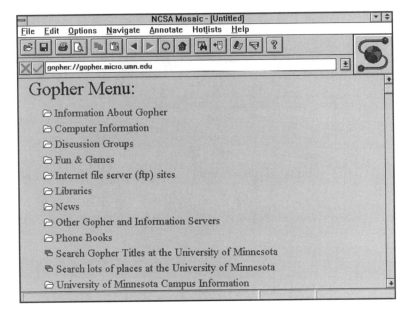

Where are all these Gophers?

Gopherspace is out there in the near and far reaches of the Internet, but where is it really? Where are these computers, and who puts information on them? And what kinds of things are out there in Gopherspace?

Real people work hard to make things available across the Internet, and Gopherspace is certainly no exception. Gopher computers are located at places like universities and companies; places with the necessary computer resources. All the software, text, graphics, and other files are there because people took the time to contribute to the growing virtual world of Gopherspace and the Internet.

Most Gopher servers are located at some sort of organized (or disorganized, for that matter) computing department. Universities, corporations, and organizations run Gopher servers as part of their computing environment. They have the staff to make files available and maintain the machines.

Each Gopher site publishes its information in its own way, setting up directories of related information as it sees most useful. Some sites are organized and straightforward; some are set up very creatively. Some sites are full of unique, new information; other sites have few unique files, but a lot of pointers to other Gopher computers.

 **<Caution>** Although Gopherspace is a lot more G-rated than other parts of the Internet, you may still encounter some files that you find inappropriate or offensive. If you don't like what you find at a site, leave it behind and visit other sites instead.

Look to Gopherspace

The part of the Internet you can burrow around in with Gopher is sometimes called Gopherspace. Gopherspace is to Gopher software what the Web is to software like Mosaic. It includes thousands of Gopher computers and other parts of the Internet like UseNet news archives and online library databases.

Within Gopherspace, Gopher can do things for you like:

- Navigate the Internet by selecting items from menus
- Retrieve and display text files
- Retrieve graphics files and launch programs to display them
- Retrieve sound and video files and launch programs to play them
- Start a Telnet connection to a remote computer
- Display UseNet news messages

From the home of the Golden Gophers

Gopher was developed at the University of Minnesota to solve a campus computing problem. There was information on different computers in different departments all over campus. Each department wanted control over the content of its computer, but people wanted access to information on all the departments' computers from anywhere on campus.

This could have been done many different ways. What the group at Minnesota came up with was a system that hid hard-to-remember address information and commands behind the Gopher simple interface.

Part II of this book teaches more about all of these things that Gopher can do. You also learn just by being online and burrowing through Gopherspace.

Schools

Gopher started at a school, so it's only fitting that a lot of universities maintain numerous Gopher severs. You'll find both official and unofficial information at universities worldwide.

Official information might include:

- Class schedules
- Campus library connections
- Archives of software tools
- Technical documents (like the description of the Gopher protocol)
- Phone books, or directories, of students, faculty, and staff
- Academic papers, reference materials, and research results

The unofficial Gopher files at universities are endless, and somewhat difficult to categorize. Different departments maintain their own servers, so let's just say the information is diverse. Though much of what's available is serious technical or academic information, a lot of it is intended to be just for fun.

Companies

Corporate Gophers may be open to the public, although it's safe to say there are plenty that are not. Companies like Microsoft, IBM, and Novell all have publicly available Gopher sites—so do numerous publishing companies and Internet service providers.

The power of Gopher's distributed system makes it easy for companies to publish internal information for their employees. Of course, it's also a great way for companies to make information available to the public as well.

Plain English, please!

A **distributed system** is one where different information resides on different computers in separate locations but is accessible to all users. Whether within a corporate network or on the Internet as a whole, Gopher is an excellent example of a distributed system.

Again, the information about a company may be official or unofficial. It could be information about the company's products, customer support files, or even things posted just for fun. It depends on the company's product, and its corporate culture.

Government agencies

Government agencies and related organizations, like the U.S. Congress, NASA, and the United Nations, maintain Gopher servers. These servers contain everything from census data to legislative records to lists of e-mail addresses for members of Congress.

The WSGopher software contains a list of U.S. Government-related Gophers. See Chapter 5, "Using Bookmarks to Save Your Place," for information on using this feature with WSGopher.

What Do I Need to Gopher?

In this chapter:

- Which Gopher software should I use?
- Where can I find WSGopher?
- Downloading WSGopher from the Net
- Getting WSGopher from an access provider
- How to install WSGopher

The WSGopher software makes navigating the Internet a breeze. Here's how to find and install it.

As my dad, the handyman, says, "The right tool for the right job." Likewise, to go gophering around the Internet, you need the right tool—good Gopher software. There are a number of Gopher programs for Windows; Appendix A, "Other Gopher Software," lists some of them.

Possibly the best Internet Gopher going is WSGopher, written by Dave Brooks from Lockheed Idaho Technologies Co. WSGopher is well-designed software and has the features to make gophering easy. It's widely available, and it's free.

This chapter will help you find a copy of WSGopher and get it installed. Although it's possible that your access provider will give you this software, you can get it from Internet FTP sites. Once you have the WSGopher software, it's easy to install and set up an icon for it in Program Manager. After that, you'll be off and gophering.

Our Favorite Gopher: WSGopher

WSGopher is widely used free with copyright Gopher software. Free with copyright means you can download it for your own use, but the software is copyrighted by the developer. WSGopher was one of the first Gophers written for Windows, and it remains one of the best Gophers around. The author of the program, Dave Brooks, still works on updates and you can send comments or questions to him at **gopher@tis.inel.gov**.

 (Tip)

> WSGopher is available for you to download and use, but if you intend to distribute it in any way, you must apply for a license from Lockheed Idaho Technologies Co. For more information, see the file announce.txt that installs with WSGopher.

You can navigate WSGopher with menu commands or a handy toolbar. You can also get a long way into Gopherspace just by pointing and clicking. In WSGopher, each new Gopher directory displays in a separate window. You can save an individual Gopher file or a whole directory into a bookmark so you can easily get back to it later.

66 *Plain English, please!*

With a printed book, a **bookmark** is a way to save your place, so you can return there easily. Bookmarks in Gopherspace work the same way. By saving a bookmark for a Gopher item, you'll be able to get back to that item without retracing your steps. Once you've explored Gopherspace, even a little, you'll understand the usefulness of this important feature. 99

WSGopher comes with a detailed set of bookmarks, organized by categories like Humor, U.S. Government Information, and Education. For more information about the bookmarks feature of WSGopher, see Chapter 5, "Using Bookmarks to Save Your Place."

WSGopher is a full MDI (Multiple Document Interface) application. You can minimize any Gopher directory and go back to it later in your session. Figure 2.1 shows WSGopher with several Gopher directories open. You can click in any window to connect to other Gopher sites or to files in that directory.

Plain English, please!

MDI, or **Multiple Document Interface**, is a Windows programming standard. Basically, it means that each Gopher directory appears in its own window, much like each document appears within its own window in an application like Microsoft Word.

Fig. 2.1
WSGopher with several Gopher directories open, each in their own window.

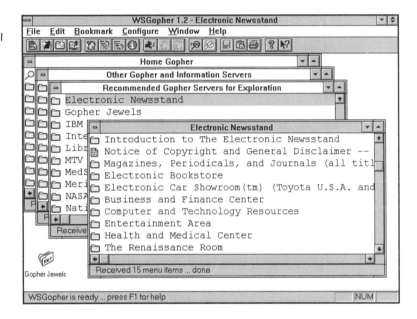

The most recent release of WSGopher is version 1.2. Part II of this book, "Starting to Use Gopher," shows you how to use the features of WSGopher 1.2. WSGopher is a great example of the kind of software you can find for free on the Internet.

First things first: finding a copy of WSGopher

To get started with WSGopher, you need to find a copy of it to run on your PC. Don't head out to the store just yet; though it might sound confusing at first, some of the best places to find Internet software are on the Internet itself.

Don't worry. On the Internet, getting a copy of a widely available product like WSGopher is really fairly easy. If you're new to the Internet, finding it may prove to be a good early lesson on using the Net. If you're used to FTP, then getting a copy of WSGopher will be easy.

Finding software on the Internet that you want to use to search the Internet is a little like pulling yourself up with your own bootstraps. However, with these directions you should be able to easily find a copy of WSGopher.

> When you find WSGopher, it probably won't be the only software you find. You may find other useful applications to download while you're getting your copy of WSGopher.

FTP WSGopher from the Net

WSGopher is available at many popular anonymous FTP sites. If you don't have a site that you use as your usual software archive, then look for it at the boombox server at the University of Minnesota. Where else would you get Gopher software?

 Plain English, please!

Anonymous FTP is a very important part of downloading software on the Internet. Certain servers will let you log in, even though you don't have an account at that site. To gain access to these computers, you log in as the user *anonymous*. Many such FTP sites ask that you use your e-mail address as your password. You can then retrieve files stored at that computer, like the WSGopher software.

> If you've never retrieved files from the Internet with FTP, you may need more information about FTP and the Internet in general. You may want to read a basic Internet book, like *Using the Internet,* or a book on FTP, like *Using FTP,* both available from Que.

To get to the Gopher software on boombox, follow these steps. You need to be somewhat familiar with anonymous FTP and have FTP software or a shell account. These instructions will help, though they're generic enough to apply to any FTP application.

1 Connect your PC to the Internet and launch your FTP software. This program may be a command-line shell account, or a point-and-click Windows application.

2 Connect your FTP software to **boombox.micro.umn.edu**. This is the address of the FTP site at the University of Minnesota.

3 Log in as anonymous and use your e-mail address as your password.

4 Switch directories to /pub/gopher/Windows. With command-line FTP, use the cd command to change directories. In Windows FTP programs, you can select the directories and double-click to open them.

5 Find the wsg-12.exe file.

6 Retrieve wsg-12.exe back to your PC. (Be sure the FTP software is set to binary and not ASCII; this isn't a text file.)

Figures 2.2 and 2.3 show some examples of FTP software connected to FTP site **boombox.micro.umn.edu**. Figure 2.2 shows a command-line connection after retrieving WSGopher. Figure 2.3 shows the Windows FTP client from the popular Internet Chameleon package ready to retrieve the WSGopher install file.

After the FTP is complete, you'll have the wsg-12.exe file on your PC. Now you're ready to continue setting up WSGopher. See the section, "How to Install WSGopher," later in this chapter.

Here are a couple of other FTP sites that archive the WSGopher software. If for some reason you can't get to the site at the University of Minnesota, check out these FTP archives for the wsg-12.exe file:

FTP to this Internet address	Go to this directory
sunsite.unc.edu	pub/micro/pc-stuff/ms-windows/winsock/apps
dewey.tis.inel.gov	pub/wsgopher

Fig. 2.2
A command-line FTP session, showing all the steps to get to the WSGopher file. Remember that UNIX is case-sensitive, and that you'll have to download the software to your PC after retrieving it through your shell account.

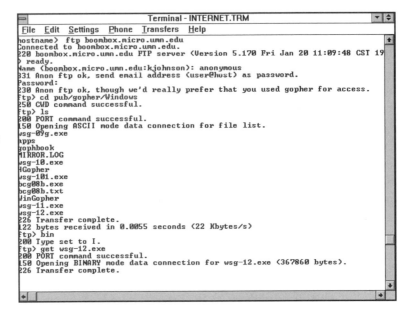

Fig. 2.3
A popular example of a Windows-based FTP program. This software is connected to the same host and directories as that shown in figure 2.2.

Click the copy button to retrieve wsg-12.exe

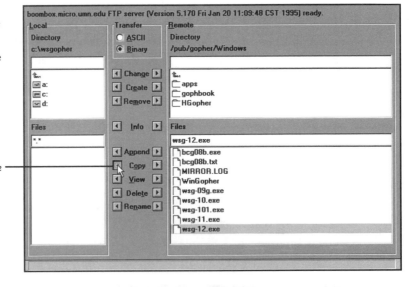

Gopher for WSGopher

If you use other Windows Gopher software, you can probably use that Gopher to retrieve WSGopher as well. Connect to the same machine, boombox at the University of Minnesota. To get there through Gopher, follow these steps:

1 Connect to the main Gopher server at the University of Minnesota (**gopher.micro.umn.edu**).

2 Select Information about Gopher.

3 Select Gopher Software Distribution.

4 Select Windows.

5 Select the wsg-12.exe file.

The Gopher software retrieves the file to your PC's hard drive.

Cruise the Web for WSGopher

If you have software for the World Wide Web, like Mosaic or Netscape, you can use that software to get WSGopher. Connect your Web browser to the following address:

ftp://boombox.micro.umn.edu/pub/gopher/Windows

Download the file wsg-12.exe by clicking on it and saving it to your hard drive.

Your local Internet Access Provider

Depending on the company who provides your Internet access, you may get a copy of WSGopher as part of an Internet startup package. Ask your provider if you're not sure. You should get some of the tools, like FTP or Gopher software, along with your connection account. These tools can help you find WSGopher and all the other software you need.

Other software that you might need are applications to play sound or video files, view image files, or connect to Telnet sessions. See Chapter 6, "Getting By with a Little Help from Your Friends," for more information.

How to install WSGopher

After you've found a copy of the wsg-12.exe file, installing WSGopher is very easy. Wsg-12.exe is a self-extracting file. When you run it, it will unpack itself and create the files needed to run WSGopher.

 Plain English, please!

A **self-extracting** file is a file that contains other files that have been compressed. When you run the self-extracting file, it decompresses them. Unlike a file that is compressed with a program like PKZIP.EXE, you don't need another application to uncompress a self-extracting file. To run it, you just double-click on the file in the Windows File Manager. 99

To install WSGopher after you find the wsg-12.exe file through FTP, follow these steps:

1 Open File Manager.

2 Create a directory for WSGopher—c:\wsgopher, for example.

3 Copy the wsg-12.exe file into that directory. Figure 2.4 shows wsg-12.exe in a directory called wsgopher.

Fig. 2.4
To install WSGopher, put wsg-12.exe in its own directory and double-click the file.

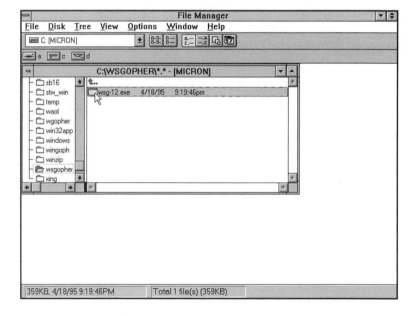

4 Double-click on the file wsg-12.exe.

Your PC switches to DOS to actually unpack the WSGopher files, and then switches back to Windows File Manager when it's finished.

5 Press F5 to refresh the File Manager window and display the WSGopher files, as shown in figure 2.5.

Fig. 2.5
After installation, you can read the announce.txt file or you can launch the program by double-clicking wsgopher.exe.

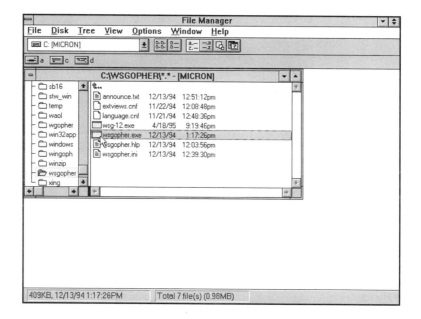

The simple install instructions here assume that you don't have an earlier version of WSGopher that you've been using. If you do have an earlier version, read the file announce.txt before you run WSGopher 1.2. The Installation section has some notes that you should read first.

After you've unpacked WSGopher, take a minute to look over the documentation in the announce.txt file. You probably won't need to read it all, but it does contain useful updates about the product.

Q&A

> ### When I double-clicked wsg-12.exe, it didn't build the files properly. What happened?
>
> You may have downloaded the file as ASCII instead of Binary. If you down-loaded the WSGopher install file from a command-line FTP session, be sure you switch to binary retrieve with the **bin** command before you get the wsg-12.exe file.

To run WSGopher, you'll want to create an icon for it in Program Manager. The fastest way to do this is to:

- Click on the wsgopher.exe file in File Manager.

- Drag it into the Program Manager group of your choice.

Before you do this, arrange File Manager so you can easily see the group where you want to put WSGopher. Figure 2.6 shows the WSGopher icon in the Program Manager group.

Fig. 2.6
Here the WSGopher icon appears in its own Program Manager group. You can drag the icon into any group you choose.

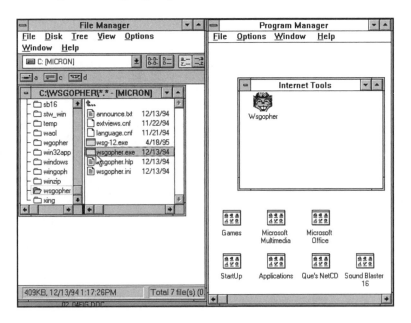

After the icon is on your desktop, you're ready to begin exploring the Internet with WSGopher.

Part II:

Starting to Use Gopher

3

Getting Started with WSGopher

Gophering is as easy as pointing and clicking. This chapter gets you going with WSGopher basics.

Now that you've found and installed the software, it's time to get started with WSGopher. This chapter gets you up and running, and walks you through a simple WSGopher session.

Starting WSGopher

Starting WSGopher is as easy as clicking on the icon; but before you do that, ask yourself a few questions:

- Do you have an account set up with an Internet access provider?

- Do you use any other Windows-based Internet software, like an e-mail program or a newsreader?

- Does your connection open up when you launch software, or do you need to open the connection first?

If you answered No or I don't know to any of these questions, then you need to know more about your Internet connection before you run WSGopher. Take a minute now and find the answers. If you need more information, check out Appendix B, "Understanding Internet Connections," or a general Internet reference book, like *Using the Internet*, published by Que.

How to launch the program

After you have your Internet connection in place, launching WSGopher is easy: double-click the WSGopher icon in Program Manager. The WSGopher window opens and the program tries to make its first connection out to Gopherspace.

The first time you launch it, WSGopher tries to connect to the Gopher server at the University of Illinois. This is simply a starting point so that WSGopher connects somewhere on the Net.

We call this first server the Home Gopher. After WSGopher has successfully launched and connected to the Home Gopher, it looks like figure 3.1. To change the Home Gopher that WSGopher connects to, see the Chapter 4 section, "There's no place like Home."

Fig. 3.1
WSGopher, connected to the University of Illinois, ready and waiting to start gophering.

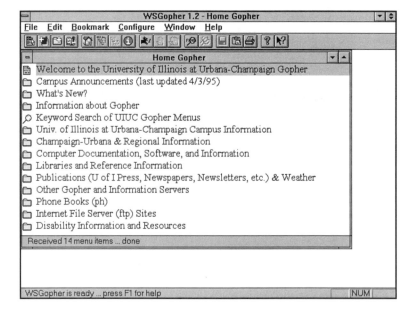

What do these messages mean?

While WSGopher is connecting the first time, it displays these messages along the bottom of the Home Gopher window:

- `resolving hostname gopher.uiuc.edu`

- `connecting to gopher.uiuc.edu`

- `sent request to gopher.uiuc.edu`

- `received 14 menu items. . . done`

If your Internet connection is open and the Gopher server at the University of Illinois—Urbana Champaign (uiuc) is running, then the first three messages will display only briefly. You may not even have time to read them.

`Resolving hostname` means that WSGopher is looking up the address to that particular Gopher site. `Connecting` means that WSGopher has found the Gopher site and is opening a connection to it. `Sent request` tells you that the connection is open and WSGopher has asked the Gopher site for information.

When the `Received 14 items. . . done` message appears, the connection is complete. Refer to figure 3.1 to see where this message appears.

These messages simply mean that WSGopher is looking up a Gopher address. You'll notice that similar messages display whenever WSGopher makes a connection.

Troubleshooting the first connection

When WSGopher can't make its first connection, it displays two error messages and then offers to let you name a new Gopher server to connect to when WSGopher launches. Figure 3.2 shows the first of these error messages.

Fig. 3.2
This error message tells you that WSGopher couldn't get to a Gopher server.

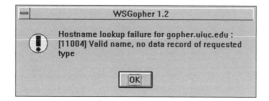

To clear this message box, just click OK or press Enter. WSGopher then tells you it was unable to reach the Home Gopher server (see fig. 3.3).

Fig. 3.3
WSGopher lets you know that it couldn't connect to your Home server.

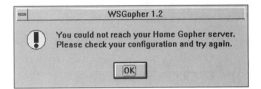

Click OK to clear this error message. Now WSGopher gives you a chance to change the Home server, as shown in figure 3.4. At this point, just close this dialog box by clicking Cancel.

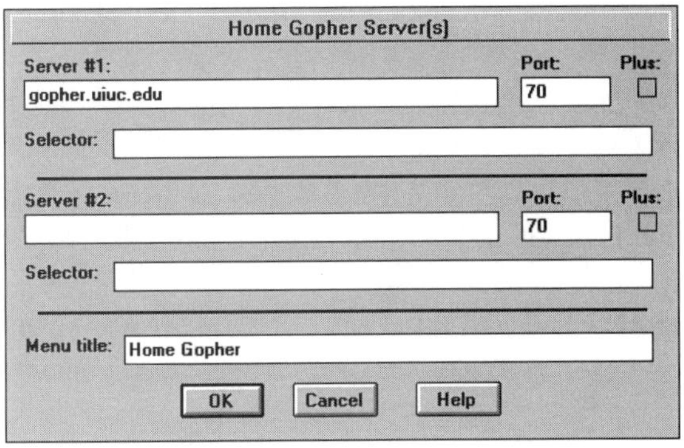

Fig. 3.4
If WSGopher can't connect to the Home Gopher, it offers to let you change servers. Check your Internet connection first.

There are a couple of simple reasons why WSGopher might not make its first connection:

- The Gopher site is not available, or is too busy.

- Your Internet connection isn't open.

There's not much you can do if the computer at this Gopher site is down, but you can make sure your Internet connection is up and running. Check the connection and then launch WSGopher again. If your connection is open, the Gopher site may be busy; try the connection again.

(Tip)

One quick way to test your Internet connection is simply to open another application. Launch your e-mail program, for example. After it's connected, try WSGopher again.

If, for some reason, the server is not available, and your connection is open, you'll still be able to go gophering. You can use the WSGopher Bookmarks menu to begin searching. See Chapter 5, "Using Bookmarks to Save Your Place," for more on how to do that.

The WSGopher Window

Okay, you have your Internet connection in place and you've found WSGopher at an FTP site. You've installed and launched it, and now you're ready to go. Let's take a look at the WSGopher window from top to bottom.

Title bar

As with most Windows applications, the title bar appears at the top of the window. With WSGopher, it displays:

- Name of the application (WSGopher)

- Version number (1.2)

- Title of the current Gopher window, if one is open

The name of the directory in the title bar changes as you navigate Gopherspace. It may help you find your place if the Gopher directory area gets too crowded.

Menu bar

Below the title bar is the menu bar. The menus contain the commands used to run WSGopher. It contains the following menus:

- File

- Edit

- Bookmark

- Configure

- Window

- Help

What's all this stuff on the screen?

Fetch button
Tell WSGopher to fetch the
selected item with this button.

WSGopher title bar
This bar displays the name of
the current Gopher directory
and the version of WSGopher
you're using.

Cancel or stop buttons
Stop single or multiple WSGopher
retrievals with these two buttons.

Menu bar
The menus list all the
commands and options
of WSGopher.

Toolbar
The toolbar
provides
easy access
to some
commands.

WSGopher 1.2 - University of Minnesota Gopher Server, Home of the Gopher

File   Edit   Bookmark   Configure   Window   Help

Home Gopher
Other Gopher and Information Servers
Recommended Gopher Servers for Exploration
University of Minnesota Gopher Server, Home of the Gopher

Information About Gopher
Computer Information
Discussion Groups
Fun & Games
Internet file server (ftp) sites
Libraries
News
Other Gopher and Information Servers
Phone Books
Search Gopher Titles at the University of Minn

Received 12 menu items ... done

All the Gopher   Other Gopher
Servers in the   and Information
World   Servers

WSGopher is ready ... press F1 for help   NUM

Content area
This area shows
all the open
Gopher direct-
ories, including
directories
minimized as
icons along the
bottom.

Directory status bar
The status bar for each
directory tells you how
many items there are in
that directory, and if
WSGopher is still retrieving
them, or is done.

Main status bar
This bar tells you
about menu items
or toolbar buttons
you select.

Menu item text
The text that follows
the icons describes
each Gopher item.

Icons
These icons tell you what kind of
item this is (directory, text file,
image file, and so on).

Each menu contains various commands under that heading. When you place the cursor over a menu command, a brief description appears in the status bar at the bottom of the window. Later chapters will describe the menu commands and options in more detail.

Toolbar

The toolbar, shown in figure 3.5, contains a set of buttons that provide a shortcut to some commands. These commands can also be performed with menu commands. The toolbar simply makes it easier.

Fig. 3.5
These toolbar buttons help you navigate with WSGopher.

Here's a quick summary of what each toolbar button does:

Opens the Fetch Bookmark dialog box

Saves the selected item as a bookmark

Saves the entire directory as a bookmark

Opens the Bookmark Editor

Connects to your Home Gopher

Goes to the top level of the current Gopher

Goes up one level in the current Gopher

Opens the Item Information window

Fetches the selected Gopher item

Cancels the most current WSGopher action

Cancels all WSGopher actions

 Finds text in a Gopher directory window

 Finds the next occurrence of text

 Saves the current item

 Copies the current item

 Prints the current item

 Shows information about WSGopher

 Activates WSGopher's context sensitive Help

 To use WSGopher's context-sensitive Help, click on that toolbar button. You'll notice that a question mark now appears over the cursor. Click on any part of the WSGopher window, or choose a menu item, and WSGopher displays the appropriate Help topic.

To see a description of a button on the toolbar, click on it and hold the mouse button down. A brief description appears on the status bar at the bottom of the window. If you move the pointer away from the button before releasing your mouse button, you won't activate the button. The WSGopher Help file also has a topic, called Overview of Toolbar, that identifies each button.

Gopher directories

The main part of the window is where WSGopher displays each of the Gopher directories in a separate window. As WSGopher opens new directories, they cascade from the upper left of this area to the bottom right. If you minimize a window, the icon also appears along the bottom of this part of the window. If you maximize a window, it fills this entire area.

Status bar

The status bar appears at the bottom of the WSGopher window. Most of the time it simply says WSGopher is ready. . . press F1 for help. When you select a menu item, or click a toolbar button, this is where the description appears. On the right side of the status bar, WSGopher tells you if you have turned on the Num Lock, Caps Lock, and Scroll Lock settings for your keyboard.

The contents of a Gopher server

When WSGopher connects to a Gopher server, the server presents a list of things. When you select something from that list, WSGopher goes for it and brings it back to you. The kinds of things listed in Gopher directories are:

- Other directories
- Files

This is a short list, but within these two simple categories is a lot of information. The directories provide the structure of Gopher; the files provide the information and entertainment. You navigate from directories of directories to directories of files.

The real advantage of Gopher servers and the Internet is that a Gopher directory can contain things that aren't really at that site at all. That is, not all of the directories or files listed in a Gopher directory need to be on the same machine. They don't even have to be on the same continent!

An obvious example is the directory called All the Gopher Servers in the World. Many Gophers have a link to this directory, and it actually resides at the University of Minnesota. But when you connect to any of the Gopher sites listed in this directory, WSGopher makes the connection to wherever in the world that Gopher is.

As a Gopher user, you don't even need to know whether an item listed on a Gopher server is really stored on that server or not. Gopher retrieves it for you from wherever it is. Connections halfway around the world may take a little longer, but Gopher will get you there.

Gopher directories

WSGopher displays the contents of each directory in a new window (see fig. 3.6). The directory may be a whole new server, or just another directory on the same machine.

Fig. 3.6
A WSGopher directory window. Each directory window displays its own status information.

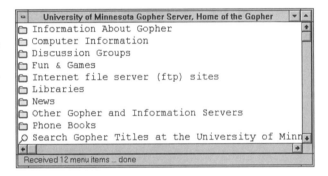

The window title bar tells you the name of the directory. The icons and text in the window describe each of the items in the new directory. The status bar tells you the number of items in the directory, and whether WSGopher is still retrieving them, or is finished.

WSGopher uses the term *fetch* instead of retrieve. You can tell WSGopher to fetch a Gopher item three ways.

- Double-click the item in the directory window.

- Select the item by clicking it, and then click the Fetch button.

- Select the item and choose <u>F</u>ile, Fetch Item.

When you tell WSGopher to fetch an item in a Gopher directory, WSGopher reads the information in the bookmark for that item. It then uses the bookmark information to connect to the item, wherever it is on the Internet.

Plain English, please!

A **bookmark** is something that helps you keep your place. WSGopher uses the term bookmark to refer to all items that display at a Gopher server. Each bookmark is actually a pointer to the item on the Internet. With WSGopher, you can save the bookmark for any item in Gopherspace and get back there easily. For more information on bookmarks, see Chapter 5, "Using Bookmarks to Save Your Place.

 WSGopher identifies each item in a directory with an icon. In WSGopher, directories are shown as file folders, which is an apt description, because like a file folder, directories can contain different kinds of files or even other Gopher directories. The text description next to the icon in the WSGopher window tells you something about the contents of the directory.

Gopher files

Besides lists of directories, there are files in Gopherspace: text files, images, sounds, videos, software, and connections to other computers. Chapter 1, "The Why, What, and Where of Gopher," talks about the kinds of things you'll find with Gopher. You'll encounter all these types of files after you start gophering.

Just as it represents directories with a file folder icon, WSGopher represents each type of file with a unique icon. The WSGopher Help file lists all of the different icons, but here are the most common ones.

 Gopher directory

 Gopher text file

 Image file, probably in either GIF or JPG format

 Gopher index search interface

 Movie file probably in MPEG or QuickTime format

Sound file

 Telnet login session (WSGopher launches a Telnet client to actually connect to the session)

The longer you cruise around the Internet with WSGopher, the more of these file types you're likely to encounter. See Chapter 6, "Getting By with a Little Help from Your Friends," for more about file types and how WSGopher works with them. The next section gives you a brief introduction to Gopher searching.

A brief burrow

So much for talk. As with any Internet software, it's easier to show how Gopher works than talk about it. Let's look at a brief session. We'll go looking for the Gopher Protocol document which is a technical description of Gopher that starts out with an amusing dictionary definition.

Starting from Home

Like many journeys, this one starts from Home. In this case, Home is the Gopher at the University of Illinois, defined as the Home Gopher when you first launch WSGopher (see fig. 3.7).

We're looking for a document that describes Gopher, so let's try the directory Information about Gopher and see where that gets us. When we double-click on Information about Gopher, we get the directory shown in figure 3.8.

 Well, Gopher was first developed at the University of Minnesota, so let's connect to the directory Gopher Protocol Documentation (from U Minn.). Double-click that item, or select it and click the Fetch button to get WSGopher to retrieve it. Figure 3.9 shows us the Gopher items in that directory.

Fig. 3.7
Home is a good place
to start.

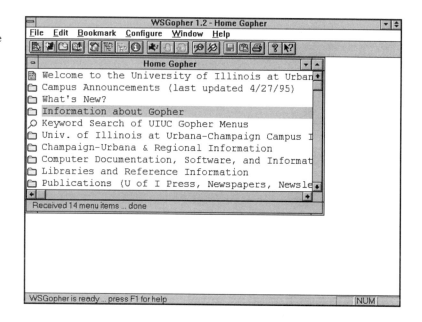

Fig. 3.8
A double-click on
Information about
Gopher brings up the
Information about
Gopher directory
window, that displays a
list of likely directories
and files.

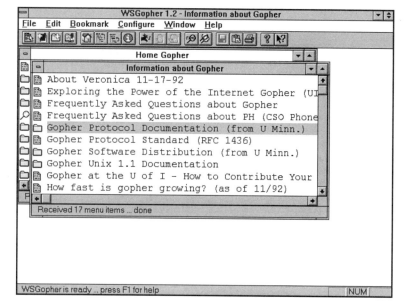

Fig. 3.9
Minnesota is where Gopher got started, so it seems a likely place to look for information about Gopher.

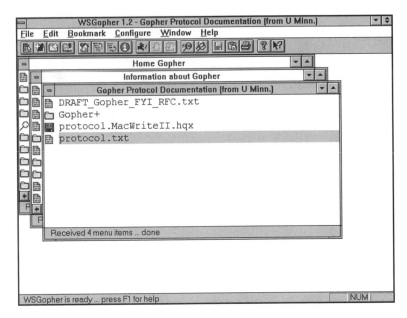

Getting to the University of Illinois Gopher

When you first install and launch WSGopher, it connects to the University of Illinois Gopher. If you've changed that, or if you're using different Gopher software, here's the address of the U of I Gopher. (These fields match the Fetch This Gopher Item dialog box in WSGopher.) To open this dialog box choose File, New Gopher Item.

Title: University of Illinois at Urbana-Champaign
Server name: **gopher.uiuc.edu**
Server port: 70

Selector:
Item Type: Directory
URL: **gopher://gopher.uiuc.edu/>**

See Chapter 4, "Navigating Gopherspace," for more information about gophering by address with WSGopher. If you are using different Gopher software, enter the address in the appropriate dialog box for that program. Remember, a Gopher directory is File type=1.

Plain English, please!

Figure 3.9 shows several new Gopher items. A file ending in **.txt** is a text file; WSGopher displays it in its own window. A file ending in **.hqx** is a compressed binary file of a MacWriteII document. If you're using WSGopher and a PC, you won't want that format.

Gopher+ is a set of extensions to the original Gopher protocol. It allows Gopher servers to give more information about Gopher items and provides a way for Gopher users to send information back to servers. The directory shown in figure 3.9, as well as the WSGopher Help file, will give you more information about Gopher+. **"**

Hmm, there are four choices shown in the window in figure 3.9. We're looking for a document on the Gopher protocol, so let's try the file protocol.txt. Double-click the item protocol.txt and WSGopher displays the file shown in figure 3.10 in a text window.

Fig. 3.10
We've found our file about the Gopher protocol.

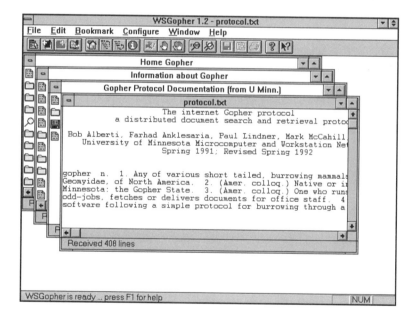

Figure 3.10 displays the document we were looking for. It also lets us look back at the path we traveled, something sometimes useful to do. WSGopher opened each new directory in its own window and cascaded each window so we can easily see how we got to the protocol.txt document.

Admittedly, I knew where I was leading you, and we took a pretty straight path to get there. Still, this simple search should give you an idea of how you'll get around Gopherspace with WSGopher.

4 Navigating Gopherspace

This chapter takes you to the Net with WSGopher, shows you what's there, and brings you home again.

In this chapter:

- Burrowing through the Net
- Connections to everywhere
- You can go home again
- Getting what you came for

Now that you've seen a brief introduction to WSGopher, let's take a closer look at how to get around Gopherspace. Remember that the Internet is like a lot of connected libraries. This chapter will show you how to get around those libraries.

Once you're more familiar with Gopherspace, you'll learn which library to go to for specific information, which library has the best staff to help you find things, and which has the best reference desk. It's all out there. Other chapters of this book will also help you find your way around Gopherspace. Check out the chapters in Part III, "Finding What You Want with Gopher," and Part V, "Finding Cool and Useful Gophers," for more direction.

Cruising the Net

Like using training wheels on your bike before you really learn to ride, you need to give yourself time to get familiar with the Net. You certainly won't find everything in Gopherspace just by hunting around, but after you get connected, give yourself time to just check it out and get a feel for it.

After you're comfortable with it, you can begin to search the Internet for specific information. All these connections can be a little confusing at first. Think of a Gopher menu as the table of contents to that Gopher site. For each directory you open, WSGopher displays the table of contents for that directory. Simple enough.

Unlike typical TOCs, however, Gopher menus contain items that aren't even on the same computer. Sort of like opening *Time* magazine and seeing that the TOC points to an article from *Newsweek*. Only, if this were true with magazines, you'd still have to go and get the copy of *Newsweek* yourself. With Gopher, there's a link from *Time* to *Newsweek*, but you don't even need to know that. When you double-click the item in the Gopher menu, Gopher goes and gets the article.

Just point and click

The real power of any Gopher software, and of the Internet in general, is that you can potentially get to anywhere from anywhere. One Gopher directory can connect you to any other Gopher, if it has the proper link. You can jump from a server at the University of Minnesota to a server in California with just a double-click.

With WSGopher you just point the cursor at an item in a Gopher menu and double-click. WSGopher goes and gets that item, whether it's another directory, a text file you want to read, or some other type of file.

As you point and click around the Internet, WSGopher opens new directory windows. Each window opens slightly below and to the right of the previous one. When its main window fills up, WSGopher starts back at the top left of its main window. If you minimize any window, the icon appears at the bottom of the main WSGopher window.

Plain English, please!

A **link** is another term for a bookmark: the address information that allows WSGopher to connect to a file or directory. Links let Gopher menus point to directories on entirely different computers. All you have to do to get there is select the item in WSGopher. **"**

Figure 4.1 shows a Gopher search that started at the Home Gopher at the University of Illinois and ended up at the University of North Carolina, where the SunSITE software archives are. Notice the SunSITE icon in the bottom left of the WSGopher window.

Fig. 4.1
A quick trip through Gopherspace allows you to retrace your path from this server in North Carolina back to your Home Gopher.

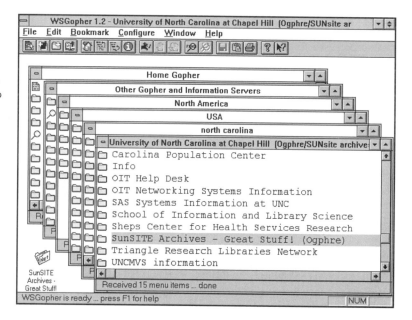

As you're navigating with WSGopher, you can close windows that you don't think you'll need again and minimize those you might like to go back to. See Chapter 5, "Using Bookmarks to Save Your Place," for more information about saving your place in Gopherspace.

Navigating by address

You don't have to get around Gopherspace just by pointing and clicking until you find what you want. If you know the address of a particular Gopher site, you can go directly there by giving WSGopher that address.

For example, there's a Gopher at the University of Southern California (USC). To get there, you can go to Other Gopher and Information Servers, USA, California, and so on.

There's got to be a quicker way, you think. There is. The Gopher at USC has a specific Internet address, like all other Gopher sites. So, if I tell you that the address is:

gopher.usc.edu

then you can get to this Gopher quickly by entering that address in WSGopher. To enter the address for a new Gopher site with WSGopher, follow these steps:

1 Choose <u>F</u>ile, <u>N</u>ew Gopher Item from the menu bar.

WSGopher opens a dialog box titled Fetch this Gopher Item, shown in figure 4.2.

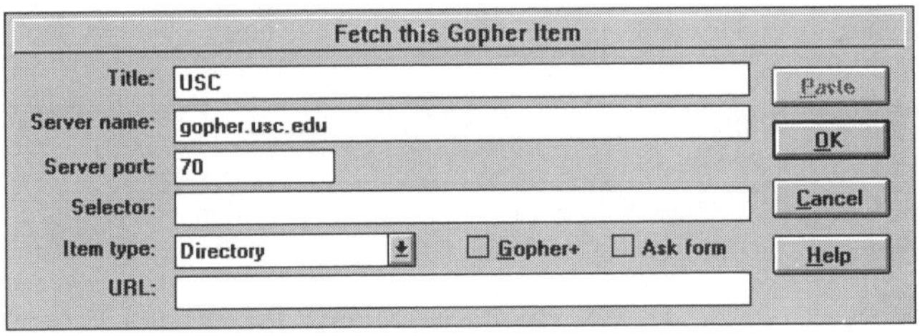

Fig. 4.2
Enter the USC Gopher address in the Server name text box and use any name you want as the title.

2 Enter a name for this Gopher in the Title text box. This is the name WSGopher displays in the directory window. Let's call it simply USC, but you can name it anything you like.

3 Enter the Gopher address in the Server Name text box. Be sure to enter it exactly: **gopher.usc.edu**.

4 Press OK.

WSGopher connects directly to the USC Gopher, shown in figure 4.3, without going through the whole state of California to get there. For more information about the Fetch this Gopher Item dialog box, and Gopher addresses in general, see Chapter 5.

Fig. 4.3
The Gopher at USC, after a direct connection.

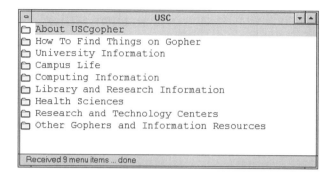

If you know the address information of any item in Gopherspace, you can use the File, New Gopher Item command to tell WSGopher to fetch that item. Just be sure to enter the address information carefully. One mistake in any field makes the address meaningless to WSGopher.

Start at the Mother Gopher

The Gopher server at the University of Minnesota is sometimes referred to as the **Mother Gopher** because Gopher was invented there. This server at the University of Minnesota contains a lot of information about Gopher, and has links to lots of other Gopher servers. On it you can find:

Not everyone starts at the top

To connect WSGopher to the top-level Gopher menu at that site, all you need to know are the server's address and title.

However, what if you want to connect to a Gopher menu that isn't the top-level menu? In these cases, you need to know the path to the item as well as the server's address. In the Fetch this Gopher Item dialog box, shown in figure 4.2, the path is called the Selector.

For example, if you want to connect to a directory of interesting Gopher links at USC called Gopher Jewels, instead of the main USC Gopher directory, you would add the following path after Selector in figure 4.2:

**1/Other_Gophers_and_Information_
Resources/Gopher-Jewels**

If you add this path and click OK, WSGopher connects directly to the Gopher Jewels directory.

- Information about the Gopher protocol

- Gopher software

- Long lists of Gopher sites

- Connections to libraries

- Lists of FTP sites

- Searching tools

The Mother Gopher can be a good place to start exploring Gopherspace. You can find resources there, as well as links to Gopher sites all over the world. You can get there two ways: by pointing and clicking, or by entering its address directly.

Find Mother Gopher by pointing and clicking

To get there from the default WSGopher Home server, point and click through these directories, starting with Other Gopher and Information Servers, shown in figure 4.4.

Fig. 4.4
The Other Gopher and Information Servers directory leads you to other Gophers at the University of Illinois and all over the Internet.

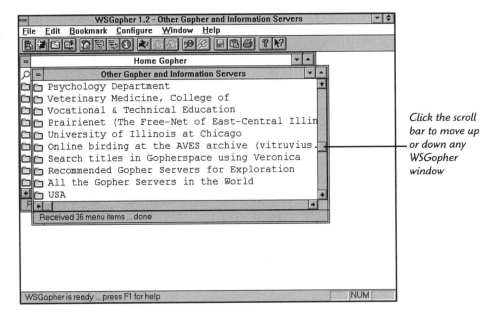

Click the scroll bar to move up or down any WSGopher window

From Other Gopher and Information Servers, double-click the Recommended Gopher Servers for Exploration directory. You'll have to scroll down from the window to see this item. Figure 4.5 shows you the contents of the Recommended Gopher Servers for Exploration directory.

Fig. 4.5
The Mother Gopher at the University of Minnesota is the first item in the Recommended Gophers directory.

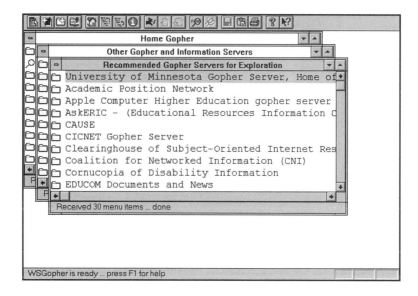

This example shows how to get to the Gopher site at the University of Minnesota from the WSGopher default Home server at the University of Illinois. As you explore Gopherspace, you'll find that many Gopher directories have links that point back to Minnesota.

Find Mother Gopher by her address

To get to the Mother Gopher without pointing and clicking all over the place, enter its address with the New Gopher Item command. Choose File, New Gopher Item and enter the name, **University of Minnesota**, and address, **gopher.micro.umn.edu**, as shown in figure 4.6, and click OK. WSGopher fetches the Mother Gopher's main directory, shown in figure 4.7.

Fig. 4.6
With this name and address, WSGopher fetches the Mother Gopher.

Fig. 4.7
The Mother Gopher
at the University of
Minnesota is a great
place to start exploring
Gopherspace.

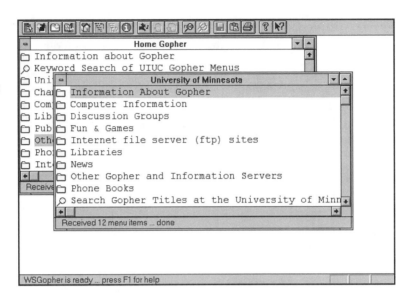

⊗<Caution> | Exploring the Mother Gopher can be rewarding, but it's a busy site. You may
not always be able to get connected. If at first you don't succeed, try again.

All the Gopher Servers in the World

You can explore Gopherspace through a directory at the University of
Minnesota's Gopher server, called All the Gopher Servers in the World.
Really. Figure 4.8 shows it with 483 directories retrieved, and many more to
follow. There are over 2,000 items in this directory.

● (Tip) | Although the All the Gopher Servers in the World directory is at the University
of Minnesota, you'll find links to it from many places in Gopherspace. The
same is true with other directories at Minnesota—many sites have links that
point back to them as well.

Fig. 4.8
All the Gopher Servers in the World takes a minute to retrieve, as you might imagine. Here WSGopher has retrieved 438 items and counting.

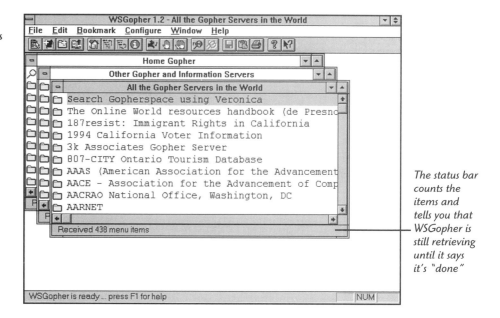

The status bar counts the items and tells you that WSGopher is still retrieving until it says it's "done"

All the Gopher Servers in the World actually lists all the Gopher servers that have sent their names and address information to the University of Minnesota. The directory lists over 2,000 Gophers alphabetically. If you know a Gopher site is out there, but you don't know where, you can start here.

Fetching more than one thing at a time

WSGopher fetches the contents of many directories quickly. However, you might have to wait while WSGopher fetches a particularly large directory, like All the Gopher Servers in the World; or a very remote directory, like one from somewhere halfway around the world.

You could just get up from your computer and take a break while WSGopher finishes these long retrieves. But you could also go on exploring Gopherspace by simply double-clicking another

Gopher item. WSGopher will retrieve multiple items at the same time.

WSGopher doesn't bring the window to the front when it finishes a retrieve. You can keep an eye on the retrieve in the background by watching its status bar. Although ultimately your Internet connection and modem speed have a lot to do with how fast WSGopher works, being able to do multiple retrieves makes using WSGopher quicker and more convenient.

When you're looking for a specific item in a large directory, like All the Gopher Servers in the World, use the Find command. To select this command, choose <u>E</u>dit, <u>F</u>ind, press Ctrl+F, or click the Find button.

Enter the text you're looking for and click OK. If the term is in the current directory, WSGopher will find it for you. See Chapter 7, "Other Gopher Activities," for more about WSGopher's Find command.

You can get to All the Gopher Servers in the World by opening the Other Gopher and Information Servers directory at the University of Minnesota (refer to fig. 4.3). You can also get there by choosing the Other Gopher and Information Servers directory from the default WSGopher Home server at the University of Illinois. Both of these two Gopher menus, and many others out there in Gopherspace, contain links to All the Gopher Servers in the World.

Gopher by geography

The University of Minnesota's Other Gopher and Information Servers directory also lists Gopher servers by where they are in the physical world. The directory lists Gophers first by continent, then by country, then by state or province.

The directories that list Gophers by geography are available from sites other than Minnesota. For example, you can get to these directories through the Other Gopher and Information Servers directory at the University of Illinois, WSGopher's default Home server. Many other Gopher sites also have links to some or all of these geographical Gophers.

So, if you know where in the world the server is, you can get to it through this directory. To find the software archives at the University of Michigan's GOpher Blue Service for example, you'd start with North America, then go to the United States, then to Michigan.

The GOpher Blue Service software archives contain a lot of different software that you can download. Free software is always a good deal, and here's a great site to look for some. Help yourself.

To track down the GOpher Blue directory, let's start from the WSGopher default Home Gopher at the University of Illinois. Find the directory Other Gopher and Information Servers and take it from there.

From here, open the USA directory and keep looking. Figure 4.9 shows the Windows software archive directory at the GOpher Blue server. Can you get there?

Fig. 4.9

The Windows archive at GOpher Blue. From the USA directory, choose Michigan, then University of Michigan GOpher Blue, then Software Archives to find your way here.

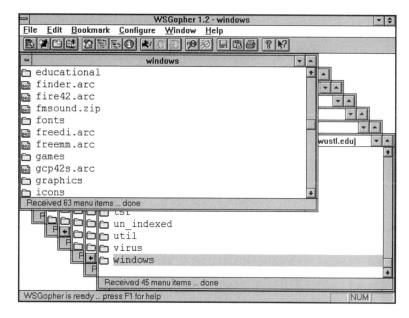

Do all these long lists and geography sound daunting? WSGopher comes with a set of predefined links to popular Gopher sites. Check out Chapter 5 for more information about them. As in the real world, if you know where you're going, it's easier to get there.

There's no place like Home

The concept of having a Home Gopher server is very important. The Home server is simply the server that WSGopher connects to each time it launches. It's also an easy place to get back to after you've completely turned yourself around and don't know where in Gopherspace you are. No matter how lost you get, you can head home with the click of a button.

WSGopher first connects to a predefined Home server, the Gopher server at the University of Illinois at Champaign-Urbana. But that may not be the best Home Gopher for you.

Your very own Home Gopher

When deciding on your Home Gopher, here are a couple of things to consider:

- Is the server reliable and easy to connect to?
- Are the links on the server useful to you?

There's no sense defining a Home Gopher that is too busy for you to get a connection each time you try; or one that is often down because of maintenance. The importance of the Home server is to get you connected at the beginning of each session and to help start you on your searches of Gopherspace.

Besides reliability, choose a server that has links that are useful to you. Some possibilities are:

- Your access provider
- Your school, business, or organization
- Your favorite topic
- Any nearby Gopher server

If your access provider maintains a Gopher server, that's useful because they may update information about their service, or post other software and files.

If your company, school, or organization runs a Gopher server, connecting to it at start-up makes sense because there's probably some useful local information there. Plus, you may be able to talk the server administrator into adding links to your favorite sites.

If you use the Internet for research on a specific topic, you may want to choose a server that specializes in information about that topic.

If you can't decide on one, choose a Home Gopher by going to the All the Gopher Servers in the World directory and finding one that's nearby. In most cases, a close proximity connection is a fast connection. Or you can just leave the Home Gopher set to the default of the University of Illinois.

Going Home

WSGopher connects to your Home server each time you launch it. Each Gopher session begins at Home and branches out from there.

 As you'll soon find out, Gopher can branch, branch, and branch again until you're not sure how you ended up wherever it is that you are. It may be time to head home and tread some familiar waters. Just click the Home button or choose File, Home Gopher, and you'll return to your Home Gopher site.

If you like where you are, you can save your place to get back there with a bookmark. See Chapter 5 for how to save your place in Gopherspace.

Change to a different Home Gopher

After you've found a Gopher site that you want to be your new Home, you'll need to know the Gopher address of the server to define it as your Home server. Let's use the Gopher server at USC as an example. To find the address of a Gopher site:

1 Navigate to that site so that it is the active window in WSGopher.

 2 Choose File, Info on Item, or click the File Information button.

The Info on Gopher Item dialog box appears, as shown in figure 4.10. (Chapter 5 describes this window in more detail.)

3 Make a note of the information in the Host and Path lines. (There may not be any information after Path; if so, you don't need to enter a Path.)

4 Click the Close button to close this dialog box.

5 Choose Configure, Home Gopher Server.

The Home Gopher Server(s) dialog box displays, as shown in figure 4.11.

Fig. 4.10
The Info on Gopher Item dialog box displays the address information for any item in Gopherspace.

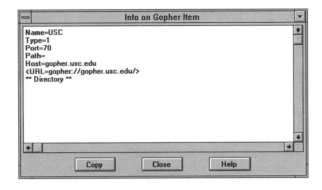

Fig. 4.11
This dialog box lets you define your Home Gopher. You can name it whatever you want, and also define a secondary server if you think your Home server #1 won't always be available.

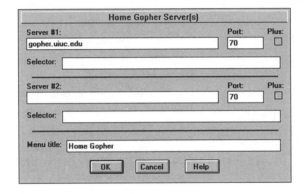

6 Enter the information from the Host line into the text box below Server #1.

7 Enter the information (if any) from the Path line into the text box after Selector.

8 Click OK to save the changes and define your new Home Gopher.

⊗<Caution> You must enter the address information exactly as it appeared in the Info on Gopher Item dialog box. If you enter it incorrectly, WSGopher will not be able to connect to your Home Gopher.

How to retrieve a file

Okay, you've now seen several ways to get around Gopherspace: ways to move from directory to directory, to jump to a specific directory if you know

its address, and how to get back to a starting place if you get too far afield.
Now let's look at the result of a Gopher search—retrieving files.

You tell WSGopher to retrieve a file the same way you tell it to retrieve a
directory. Double-click the item, or select it and click the Fetch button, and
WSGopher goes to work.

You've seen that when WSGopher retrieves the contents of a directory, it
displays them. What does WSGopher do when it retrieves a file? Well, it
depends on the type of files it retrieves.

The most common type of file in Gopherspace is probably text. When
WSGopher retrieves a text file, it simply displays the file in a new text
window, as figure 4.12 shows. To read a file in a text window, you can use the
Page Up and Page Down keys, the up and down arrows, or click the scroll
bars to page through the document.

Fig. 4.12
The introduction to
the Electronic
Newsstand, displayed
in a WSGopher text
window.

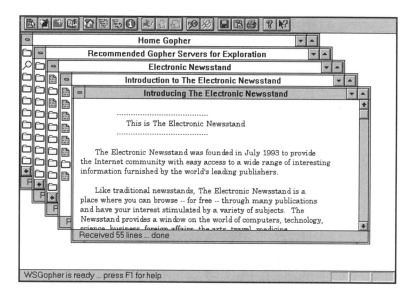

For other file types, however, Gopher just goes and gets them. It lets other
applications, called helpers, actually display or run the files.

What's a helper application?

Helper applications are programs that play or display the files that WSGopher hands off to them. Chapter 6, "Getting By with a Little Help from Your Friends," talks about helper applications in detail. The most common types of helper applications are called **viewers**. Viewers are programs that display image files, or play sound and video files. Other helper applications are Telnet and TN3270 programs that allow you to log in as a terminal on a remote computer.

When WSGopher retrieves a file, it looks at the file's extension (the part of the file name after the dot) to see what kind of file it is. Then WSGopher checks its configuration information to see if a helper application is defined for this file type.

If there's not one, WSGopher checks the File Manager associations to see if an application is defined there to handle this type of file. If a helper application is defined, WSGopher launches that application to display the file.

The download dialog box

While WSGopher is downloading a file, it displays the download dialog box, shown in figure 4.13. This dialog box provides several pieces of information:

- It identifies the file that WSGopher is retrieving.
- It reports the progress of the retrieval.
- It lets you set options for when the retrieval is complete.

Fig. 4.13

The download dialog box, after retrieving a U.S. weather map.

U.S. Weather Map
File: \u.GIF
Bytes xfer'd: 25230 bytes ... done
Xfer rate: 1.3 KBytes/sec
☒ View file when transfer is complete
☐ Save file for later use
Running 'C:\PSP\PSP.EXE \u.GIF'

While WSGopher is retrieving the file, you can select either of the two check box options:

- **View file when transfer is complete** tells WSGopher to launch a helper application when it finishes retrieving the file.

- **Save file for later use** instructs WSGopher to not delete the file when you close WSGopher.

Chapter 6 discusses helper applications in greater detail. Chapter 5, "Using Bookmarks to Save Your Place," will help you learn to save places you've found and want to return to.

 Q&A

I retrieved a file, but WSGopher displayed it as gibberish in a text window. What's wrong?

The file may be defined as an incorrect type. For example, maybe you were expecting it to be an image file, but it had a text file icon next to it.

You might be able to get the file correctly by using the Fetch Item As command. Select the item in the menu and choose File, Fetch Item As. In the dialog box that opens, change the Item Type field to the appropriate kind of file. In the example here, you'd change the type from text file to image.

Using Bookmarks to Save Your Place

Bookmarks do more than just keep you from losing your place; they let you define the Internet to your liking.

When you're reading a book, you use a bookmark to save your place. It lets you return easily to where you left off. WSGopher saves your place on the Internet by letting you store bookmarks of Gopher items. A **bookmark** is the address information that WSGopher uses to retrieve an item. By letting you save bookmarks, WSGopher makes it easy to go back to places you've been.

If the "book" you're reading is the Internet, you're going to need more than just a single placeholder. For this reason, WSGopher organizes bookmarks into categories. Each category contains multiple bookmarks that are related in some way. You can add Gopher items or whole directories to your bookmark categories, and rearrange or reorganize your bookmarks easily.

This chapter will teach you how to save your favorite places in Gopherspace with WSGopher's Bookmark Editor. It will also show you how to use the great selection of bookmarks WSGopher already has defined. These predefined bookmarks and the ones you create yourself help you keep track of the places on the Internet you want to visit often.

Lost in Gopherspace

From your beginning forays into Gopherspace, you might imagine that you could get lost wandering around the Internet with WSGopher. The strength of WSGopher can also be its weakness. It's so easy to make connections to new sites on the Internet that sometimes it's hard to remember how to get back to something interesting or important.

Figure 5.1 shows what can happen after even a short session of checking out the Internet with WSGopher and not keeping track of where you're going.

Fig. 5.1

Now how did I get here?

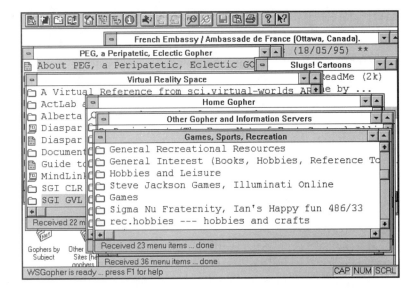

On the plus side, every place you've been is still there. WSGopher can open many Gopher directories at the same time. But after you begin closing windows, or exit WSGopher altogether, you may not remember the exact steps you took to get to a site you want to return to.

"Let's see," you think. "I started at Gopher Jewels, and then I opened the Personal Development and Recreation directory. No, it was the Miscellaneous Items directory. No, wait, I was at the USC Gopher." Lost in Gopherspace.

With its Bookmark features, WSGopher helps you save places you've been. This way, you can get back to interesting places easily and not stay lost.

WSGopher still makes it easy for you to get around the Internet, but the Bookmark features let you quickly save the location of any file or directory you find along the way.

Understanding bookmarks

Understanding the idea of bookmarks is really the key to understanding Gopher. Every Gopher directory is really just a collection of links. Bookmarks are references to links on the Internet.

When you select a bookmark from a Gopher menu, WSGopher goes and gets (WSGopher uses the term "fetches") the item that the bookmark points to. That item could be a directory—another set of bookmarks—or it could be a file.

To see the bookmark for any item in a Gopher directory, select the item and choose File, Info on Item.

First let's take a look at the bookmarks that are already set up in WSGopher. These are useful Gopher locations that Dave Brooks, the author of WSGopher, set up for you. You can add to these bookmarks, edit them, rearrange them, or remove them altogether. They're included to give you some useful starting places in Gopherspace.

How to fetch a bookmark

There are a couple of ways to fetch a bookmark with WSGopher. You can tell WSGopher to retrieve bookmarks in the following ways:

- Use the Fetch a Stored Bookmark dialog box

- Use the Bookmark Editor

 The easiest way to tell WSGopher to go and get a bookmark is to use the Fetch a Stored Bookmark dialog box. To open this dialog box, click the Fetch a Stored Bookmark button on the toolbar, or select Bookmark, Fetch.

WSGopher displays the Fetch a Stored Bookmark dialog box, shown in figure 5.2. This dialog box displays the category names on the left side and the titles of the bookmarks in the selected category on the right. When it first opens, only the categories display. Click on a category to see its bookmarks.

Fig. 5.2
Use these predefined categories and bookmarks to learn your way around Gopherspace.

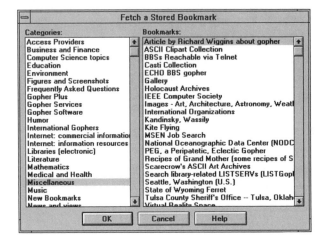

When you select a category, the bookmarks in that category appear in the list on the right. Scroll the list of categories up and down to view the bookmarks in each one. To fetch a bookmark, double-click a bookmark title.

After you tell WSGopher to go and get a bookmark, it closes the Fetch a Stored Bookmark dialog box and displays the bookmark item.

(Tip)

The Fetch a Stored Bookmark dialog box also supports keys like Page Up and Page Down, as well as the up- and down-arrow keys. To go directly to a category or bookmark, put the cursor in that list and type the first letter of the item.

You can also tell WSGopher to fetch a bookmark by using the Bookmark Editor. For more information on using the Bookmark Editor, see the section, "Don't want a certain bookmark? Delete it," later in this chapter.

❶(Tip)_____

If you often want to open more than one bookmark at once, use the Bookmark Editor, and set the User Options to leave it open after fetching. Choose Configure, User Options to open the User Options dialog. Click the checkbox in the Bookmark Editor Options section next to Keep Bookmark Editor active after fetching.

You can add your own bookmarks

The bookmarks that are predefined in WSGopher are a great way to look at the types of things out there in Gopherspace. However, Dave Brooks didn't have your exact needs in mind when he defined these categories and bookmarks. To make the Bookmarks feature of WSGopher really useful, you need to start adding your own entries. You can:

WSGopher bookmarks — ready and waiting

 WSGopher's author, Dave Brooks, includes a pretty lengthy set of bookmarks with WSGopher. These bookmarks are simply part of the WSGopher installation. You'll see them the first time you open the Bookmark Editor, or choose the Fetch a Stored Bookmark button.

You might want to use these stored bookmarks to do a little Internet exploring. Try the following categories:

Gopher Services—a list of Gopher sites that link to lots of Gopher sites, including All the Gopher Servers in the World, Gopher Jewels, Lists of FTP sites via Gopher, and more.

Education—links to Gophers at K-12 schools, an ERIC database, and the Educational Testing Service.

Miscellaneous—a little bit of everything, from interesting Gopher collections like PEG to kite flying to virtual reality. It includes image galleries from fine art to ASCII.

U.S. Government information—read the CIA World Factbook, or check out what Congress is up to, or any number of Government agencies and departments, including Voice of America news.

A quick caution: Dave Brooks includes these bookmarks as a convenience to WSGopher users. He doesn't guarantee that the sites are all inclusive, or that the information hasn't moved. These bookmarks give you great starting points, but explore on your own as well.

- Add bookmarks to existing categories

- Create new categories and add bookmarks to them

After you find the Gopher item or directory you want to save, adding a bookmark is as easy as clicking a button. WSGopher actually has two Add commands. One saves a particular Gopher item to a bookmark; the other saves the entire directory. Let's start with saving a single Gopher item.

Saving the bookmark for a single Gopher item

Keep in mind that a Gopher item can be a file or a directory, so the idea of saving a single item has more to do with how you're looking at the Gopher item than what kind of item it really is.

Let's say you're planning a trip to the American West this summer, and one of the states you'll visit is Wyoming, the Cowboy State. Before you start out on the long drive with the car packed full of gear, you should get some idea of good places to aim for. So you search the Internet for travel destinations. At a Gopher site called The State of Wyoming Ferret, you find the Gopher directory about Wyoming tourism, shown in figure 5.3.

Fig. 5.3
You can get to this server any number of ways. Check WSGopher's Miscellaneous bookmark category or just look for Gophers in the USA, then in Wyoming....

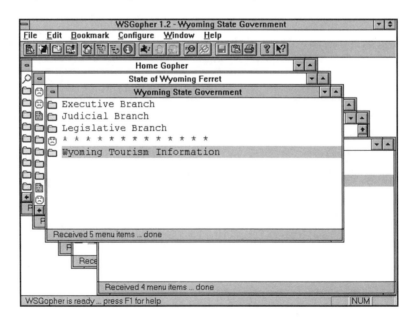

Now that you've found the Wyoming Tourism Information directory, you want to find similar directories for other Western states like Montana, Idaho, and Colorado. You decide you want to save the location of this folder so that you can come back here and check it out later. To save this single Gopher item, click the Add Bookmark button, or choose Bookmark, Add Bookmark. WSGopher opens the Select Category to Save Bookmark In dialog box (see fig. 5.4).

Fig. 5.4
To find the category you want, scroll up and down, or type the first letter of the category.

> If you want a new category for this bookmark, just enter a name in the text box and click Create. Then click OK to add the bookmark. If you click OK without first clicking Create, WSGopher asks if you really want to create the new category. If you tell it Yes, it goes ahead.

Choose a category and click OK. WSGopher saves the bookmark for this Gopher item into the category you chose.

The status line of the directory window, shown in figure 5.5, now tells you that the bookmark for Wyoming Tourism Information was successfully saved.

The bookmark to the item about traveling in Wyoming is now safely stored where you can get back to the file easily. If the file is updated, then the next time you fetch that item through WSGopher's Bookmark Editor, you'll see the new information. Now you can go see if other states have similar Gopher sites to help you plan your vacation.

Fig. 5.5
The status line always gives you up-to-the-minute information about what WSGopher is doing.

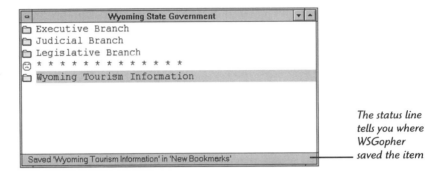

The status line tells you where WSGopher saved the item

You can save an entire Gopher directory

You've seen how to save a single Gopher item, in this case a directory of information about tourism in Wyoming. But what if you're viewing a whole directory that's worth keeping and you don't want to save every item, one at a time? WSGopher also lets you save the entire directory in one easy step.

Now let's check out travel information for the state of Utah. Sure enough, there's a Gopher site with tourist information about Utah. Figure 5.6 shows the directory and part of the path that takes you there.

Fig. 5.6
The State of Utah travel and tourism Gopher directory.

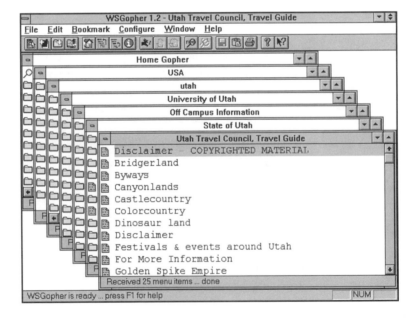

This time you've already opened the directory, but you'd like to save its entire contents. The status line tells you there are 25 items in the directory. You can save them all with one command: click the Add Directory Bookmark button or choose Bookmark, Add Directory Bookmark.

Just like when you add a single item, WSGopher asks you to pick a category for the item, then WSGopher saves the directory in that category.

Choose a default category

You may have noticed a field toward the bottom of the Select Category to Save Bookmark in dialog box called Default Category. This option lets you save bookmarks without picking a category each time.

You can also set this option by choosing Bookmarks, Categories. The dialog box is the same, it just has a different title depending on how you open it.

In either case, just select a category from the drop-down list and WSGopher automatically saves your new bookmarks to that category. You can then go back and organize them when you're not online and busy exploring the Internet.

Ways to organize your bookmarks

WSGopher organizes bookmarks into named categories. You've seen how you can fetch existing bookmarks and add new Gopher destinations to your bookmark categories. Now let's look at some of the ways WSGopher organizes your bookmarks. You can:

- Create new categories

- Rename categories

- Delete bookmarks or categories

- Move bookmarks to different categories

- Edit the name and other information of a bookmark

Create a new category

When you start saving your own WSGopher bookmarks, you'll probably want to create some particular categories to organize these Gopher items. Of course, you can always add bookmarks to any of the predefined categories as well.

To create a new category:

1 Choose <u>B</u>ookmark, <u>C</u>ategories.

The Select Category dialog box opens, as shown in figure 5.7.

Fig. 5.7

The Select Category dialog box. Doesn't it look a lot like the Select Category to Save Bookmark In dialog box shown in figure 5.4?

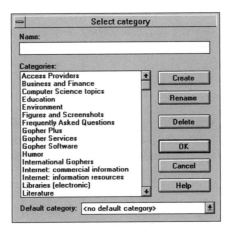

2 Enter the name of the category that you want to create in the text box at the top of the Select Category dialog box.

3 Click the Create button. The new category appears in the Categories list.

4 If you want to create more than one new category, enter the title of another one, and click the Create button.

5 Click OK to close the Select Category dialog box.

The new category, or categories, will be available for you to add newly found bookmarks the next time you're searching Gopherspace.

You can also organize bookmarks when you're offline. You can create categories and move bookmarks around among categories without being connected
to the Internet. Just launch WSGopher without your connection software
running, or close your connection without exiting WSGopher.

Give the category another name

To rename a category that already exists, follow these easy steps:

1 Choose <u>B</u>ookmarks, <u>C</u>ategories.

2 Select the category you want to rename.

3 Type the new name in the text box at the top of the dialog box.

4 Click the Rename button.

The category appears in the list under its new name. Click OK to close the
dialog box, or you can continue to reorganize your bookmark categories.

Eliminate the category

If you want to delete a category altogether, just select it and click the Delete
button. As with all good software programs, WSGopher asks if you really
want to delete this category by displaying the prompt in figure 5.8.

Fig. 5.8
If you haven't changed
your mind, just click
OK or press Enter.

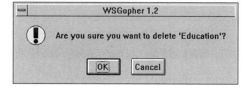

Don't want a certain bookmark?
Delete it

 To delete a specific bookmark from a category, you need to first display the
bookmarks in their category. To do this, you need to open the Bookmark
Editor. Choose the Bookmark Editor button on the toolbar or choose <u>B</u>ook-
mark, <u>E</u>dit Bookmarks.

WSGopher displays the Select Category to Edit dialog box. (This is the same Category dialog box that you've seen before; only now if you click OK, WSGopher opens the Bookmark Editor.) To continue, follow these steps:

1 Select the category that the bookmark is in.

2 Click OK.

WSGopher displays the Bookmark Editor, shown in figure 5.9.

Fig. 5.9

The Bookmark Editor not only displays each bookmark in a category, but it also shows detailed information about each bookmark.

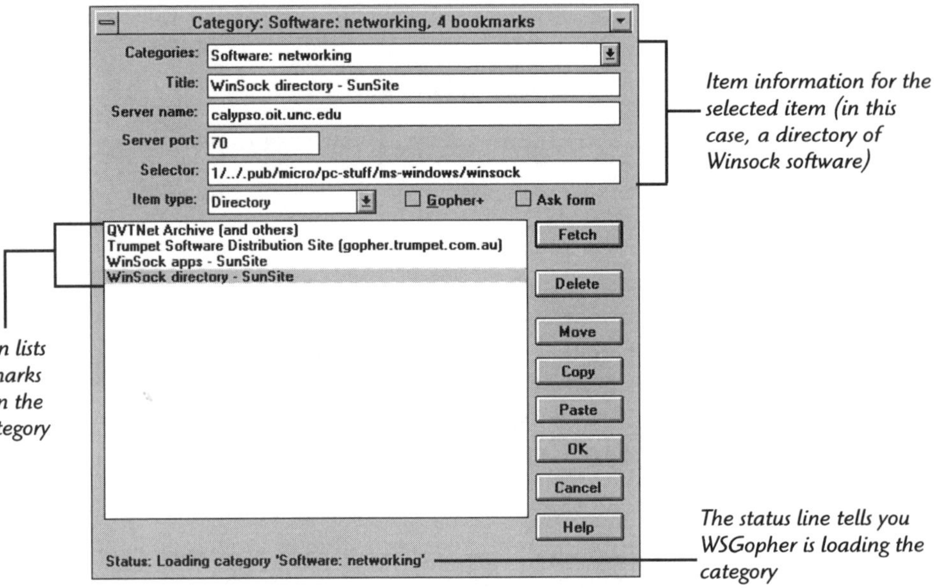

Item information for the selected item (in this case, a directory of Winsock software)

This section lists the bookmarks included in the chosen category

The status line tells you WSGopher is loading the category

The list of bookmarks for this category displays in the main part of the Bookmark Editor.

3 From this list, select the bookmark you want to delete by clicking on it.

4 Click the Delete button.

The status line at the bottom of the Bookmark Editor provides information about what WSGopher is doing, or about the last action performed by the Bookmark Editor. You can confirm a move or a deletion by checking the status line when you're working in the Bookmark Editor.

How to define a default category

After you start exploring Gopherspace you'll find plenty of places you want to go back to. As you explore, you might get tired of having to choose a category every time you want to quickly save a bookmark. Wouldn't it be nice if WSGopher would just drop all your new bookmarks in the same category so you could organize them later? It can, if you define a default category.

Defining a default category tells WSGopher to save every bookmark in the same place, without bothering you to select a category. To assign a default category, choose Bookmark, Categories. At the bottom of this dialog box, choose a default category from the drop-down list.

If you want to create a new category, like New Bookmarks, type the name in the text box at the top and click the Create button. Then choose that category as your default from the drop-down list.

Moving your bookmarks to different categories

The Bookmark Editor lets you move bookmarks to different categories easily. Let's say you have a category called New Bookmarks defined as your default category. While you're cruising around Gopherspace, you add new bookmarks to your default category.

At the end of the session, that set of New Bookmarks may be pretty diverse. When you're offline, you can use the Bookmark Editor to move bookmarks into more organized categories. To move a bookmark to another category, follow these steps:

1 Choose the Bookmark Editor button or Bookmark, Edit Bookmarks.

2 Select the category in the Categories dialog box.

3 Click OK to open the Bookmark Editor.

4 Select the bookmark you want to move by clicking on it in the list of bookmarks.

5 Click the Move button.

6 Select the category where you want this bookmark to go.

7 Click OK.

Repeat this process to move other bookmarks to other categories, or select multiple bookmarks to move more than one bookmark to the same category.

 (Tip)

> You can select multiple bookmarks at once with the standard Windows selection options:
>
> - To select bookmarks that are next to each other in the list, place the cursor over a bookmark. Hold down the left mouse button and drag the cursor up or down to select other bookmarks.
>
> - Also, to select a series of bookmarks, select the first, then hold down the Shift key and select another bookmark. This selects the first and last bookmarks, as well as all the bookmarks in between.
>
> - To select bookmarks that aren't next to each other in the list, hold down the Ctrl key while you select bookmarks. The Ctrl key works as a toggle; it selects bookmarks that aren't highlighted and unselects bookmarks that are highlighted.

Editing bookmark information

The Bookmark Editor not only lists all the bookmarks in a category, it also displays the item information for each bookmark.

❝ *Plain English, please!*

> The **item information** is the information that makes up the address that connects to a file or directory. It includes the address of the computer the item is on, the port on that computer, the path to the item, the type of item it is, and possibly more information about the item. **❞**

The item information is the address that Gopher software uses to retrieve the item from Gopherspace. As you might imagine, if you change part of the address, Gopher might not be able to locate the item.

You can edit the name of a Gopher item. This text box is used for display by Gopher software like WSGopher, and doesn't control the connection.

For the most part, you don't want to make changes in the item information that displays with the Bookmark Editor. Use the Editor simply to view this information if you're curious about where an item is in Gopherspace. You can also use the Editor to fetch bookmarks.

 (Tip)

> You can control what happens to the Bookmark Editor after you fetch a bookmark. You can set WSGopher to close the Bookmark Editor, leave it open, or minimize it. Choose <u>C</u>onfigure, <u>U</u>ser Options to open the User Options dialog box. Click the checkbox in the Bookmark Editor Options section for what you want WSGopher to do.

Share a good bookmark with friends

You may want to tell someone else about a Gopher site you have found. You could give them some general directions, like "start at the University of Minnesota's Gopher Server, then choose All the Gopher Servers in the World, then…" But wouldn't it be nice just to send them the bookmark?

With WSGopher, you can. One of the useful Gopher archives you may run into is a site called **PEG, a Peripatetic, Eclectic Gopher**. It's a set of bookmarks to other interesting Gopher sites. To send the bookmark for PEG to a friend, follow these steps:

1 Select the item in its Gopher directory.

 2 Choose the Item Information button, or select <u>F</u>ile, <u>I</u>nfo on Item.

The Info on Gopher Item dialog box opens, containing the detailed bookmark for this Gopher item. Figure 5.10 shows the bookmark for PEG.

3 Click the Copy button to copy the information to the Windows Clipboard.

4 Paste the bookmark into an e-mail message to your friend.

Fig. 5.10

If you select text, clicking the Copy button copies it. If no text is selected, clicking Copy copies the whole bookmark.

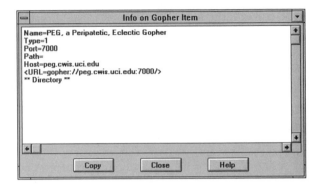

To connect to a bookmark that someone sends you, follow these steps:

1 Select the bookmark information in the e-mail message.

2 Copy it to the Windows Clipboard.

3 Open WSGopher, or switch back to it if it's already running.

4 Choose File, New Gopher Item.

5 Click the Paste button on the Fetch this Gopher Item dialog box.

6 Click OK to have WSGopher go and get the item.

Figure 5.11 shows the Fetch this Gopher Item dialog box after the bookmark for PEG was pasted in from the Windows Clipboard.

Fig. 5.11

Just click OK to connect.

①(Tip) You can paste a bookmark into the Bookmark Editor. Just open the Editor to the category where you want the new item and press the Paste button. WSGopher adds the bookmark to the category.

Your own view of the Internet

There are thousands of Gopher sites on the Internet. Just from looking at the examples you've seen so far in this book, you should realize that keeping all these Gopher sites straight is a big task. And although the menu structure of Gopher makes it easy to get around just by pointing and clicking, sooner or later you want to get somewhere just by clicking once.

WSGopher's Bookmark features allow you to customize the way the Internet looks to its most important user: you. If you are primarily interested in government information, you can organize government Gophers in more detail than the simple U.S. Government Information heading that's pre-defined.

You can subdivide the government information Gophers into more precise categories; census data, legislative records, and White House press releases could all become separate categories that help you find the information you're most interested in.

No matter what your reason for wanting access to the Internet, and no matter how interesting the process of just gophering around can be, setting up your own categories of bookmarks lets you get to the right information when you want it.

Getting By with a Little Help from Your Friends

Gopher's mission is to go and get information, but sometimes it needs help displaying what it finds. It gets that help from some friends, or helpers.

You've heard that you can retrieve images and sounds with Gopher software, but what happens to those files after you retrieve them? The team that designed Gopher built an efficient way to organize things on the Internet that lets you find and retrieve files. They gave Gopher the ability to hand files off to other software for displaying, viewing, and playing any type of file you find.

The viewers that WSGopher uses display images and files, or play sound and video files. The applications you assign as viewers are usually small programs that don't take up much memory, and primarily just display or play the file, instead of manipulating or editing them in some way.

WSGopher defines **viewers** as software that WSGopher hands files off to for displaying and playing. It leaves Telnet sessions in their own category. The term **helper applications** refers to both viewers and Telnet software.

Why does Gopher need help?

Gopher needs help because it is primarily a protocol for discovering and retrieving information. Remember, the right tool for the right job. Gopher is the right tool for going and getting things. Other software, like graphics programs and video players, are the right tools for dealing with the things Gopher gets.

This really has a couple of positive aspects. First, not having to deal with every possible file type out there keeps Gopher simpler, and lets it be good at what it does.

Secondly, and maybe more importantly, using viewers helps Gopher more easily handle new file types. Gopher only needs to know enough about a new kind of file to bring it back and find the right software to hand it off to.

For example, let's say someone creates a new image format called CIF (Cool Image Format), and files with the extension .CIF start showing up on Gophers all over the Internet. WSGopher was written before CIF files were even thought of, but if it retrieves one, it can simply hand it off to the right application to display it. Being able to hand files off to other software keeps Gopher focused on what it does best, and allows it to handle new file types easily.

Having said all that, it's important to point out that most Gopher software displays text files automatically. WSGopher simply displays the text files it receives in a window that looks much like the other WSGopher windows. But instead of a directory listing, the WSGopher text window contains, well, text.

That text could be chapters on Zen and the Art of the Internet, or a daily report on skiing conditions. WSGopher will retrieve and display text for you. You can read it online or save it to your hard drive to read later. See Chapter 7, "Other Gopher Activities," for more on saving files with WSGopher.

Though it displays text files itself, Gopher software hands off image, sound, and video files to other applications.

How to set up WSGopher helpers

There are two ways to let WSGopher know what viewer to hand off to after it retrieves a certain file type. You can configure WSGopher viewers through Windows File Manager or the WSGopher Viewers dialog box.

The Windows operating system links files and applications through **file extensions**, which are those sometimes-cryptic initials that follow a filename, like .exe, .txt, or .gif. Well, when WSGopher retrieves a file, it is smart enough to check Windows to see whether a particular program is associated with that file type.

 Plain English, please!

To **associate** means to tell File Manager that a particular file extension should be handed to a certain application. If you're not familiar with the idea of associations and file extensions, see the File Manager Help menu or the Windows documentation that came with your computer.

Some common file extensions you'll encounter in Gopherspace are listed in the following table.

Extension	File Type
.txt	Text files, handled directly by WSGopher
.gif	Image files in the Graphics Image Format
.jpg	Image files in JPEG format
.mpg	Video files in the MPEG video format
.avi	Video files in Windows AVI format
.wav	Sound files in the Wave format
.au	Sound files in AU format

You tell WSGopher where to find the Telnet and TN/3270 programs through the Telnet dialog box, accessed from WSGopher's Configure menu. The next sections walk you through setting helpers in these three ways:

- Through File Manager
- With the Viewer dialog box
- With the Telnet dialog box

Viewers and File Manager

The fastest way to set up your viewers for WSGopher will also make it easier to view files from your PC in general. After you associate file extensions with applications in Windows File Manager, WSGopher and other applications can then use those extensions to launch the right application for viewing or playing a file. Figure 6.1 shows the Windows 3.11 File Manager's Associate dialog box.

Fig. 6.1
You may be pleasantly surprised that some file types already have an application associated with them.

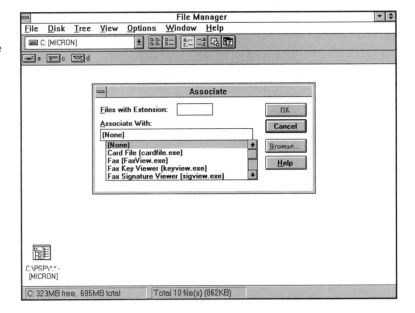

To set up file associations, follow these steps:

1 Open File Manager.

2 Select File, Associate. The Associate dialog box opens (refer to fig. 6.1).

3 Enter a file extension in the Files with Extension text box.

If a path to an application appears in the <u>A</u>ssociate With box, you're set. There is an application to handle those types of files.

4 Click OK.

 Plain English, please!

A **path** is the route that points to a file. For example, if you installed the WSGopher application in a directory called WSGOPHER on your PC's hard drive (C), the path to WSGopher is C:\WSGOPHER\WSGOPHER.EXE. When you define paths to helper applications with WSGopher, always include the executable file, which ends in .exe. **99**

To see how this works, try a common extension, like .txt for a text file, .wri for a Write document, or .bmp for a bitmap graphic. Applications such as NotePad, Write, or Paintbrush should be associated with these common file types. Enter the extension in the dialog box, and the path to the application appears.

If you enter the extension in the <u>F</u>iles with Extension text box and the <u>A</u>ssociate With field still says [None], you need to find an application that handles this file type. If you think you have the application you need on your PC's hard drive, follow these steps:

1 Click the <u>B</u>rowse button on the Associate dialog box, shown in figure 6.1. The Browse dialog box opens, as shown in figure 6.2.

Fig. 6.2
Like with an Open or Save As dialog box, you can search your hard drive from the Browse dialog box. Here we find PaintShop Pro (psp) that displays JPEG files.

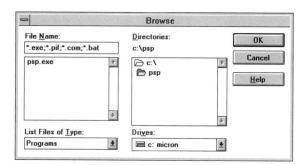

2 Find the application on your hard drive by clicking in the <u>D</u>irectories list.

3 Select the application's .exe file and click OK, or double-click the selection.

4 The Associate dialog box now shows that file extension associated with the application you chose. Figure 6.3 shows the newly defined association for the JPEG file extension, .jpg.

5 Click OK.

Fig. 6.3
PaintShop Pro (psp)
will read both GIFs and
JPEGs, so associate it
with both extensions.
Whenever WSGopher
retrieves an image file,
the file will display.

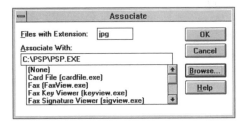

When you define file extensions through the File Manager, not only will WSGopher be able to display files of those types after it retrieves them, you can open a file just by double-clicking on it in File Manager.

Viewers in WSGopher

For certain file types, you may want WSGopher to launch a different program than you have associated in your File Manager. For example, you may have Adobe Illustrator associated with JPEG graphics through File Manager. However, you don't want WSGopher launching that large of an application every time it retrieves a JPEG graphic. Talk about overkill.

So instead of Adobe Illustrator, you'd like WSGopher to launch LView to display the JPEG files it retrieves. The WSGopher Viewers dialog box allows you to override the File Manager associations and tell WSGopher to use a particular program when it retrieves a certain file type.

Let's look at the JPEG example further. You want WSGopher to retrieve and display JPEG graphics, but you don't want WSGopher to launch Adobe Illustrator every time it goes and gets a JPEG file. You don't want to change the file extension in File Manager because you want JPEGs to open in Illustrator while you're working with them later. Here's how to set up WSGopher to override the File Manager association and use LView instead:

1 Launch WSGopher. You don't have to be connected online.

2 Choose Configure, Viewers to open the Viewers dialog box shown in figure 6.4.

Fig. 6.4
This dialog box lists the viewers you've defined, and lets you add or delete new viewers.

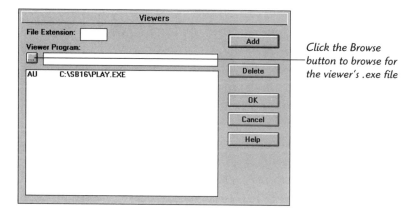

Click the Browse button to browse for the viewer's .exe file

3 Enter the file extension **JPG** in the File Extension text box.

4 Click the Browse button (refer to fig. 6.4), or type the path to the application in the Viewer Program text box.

If you click the Browse button, WSGopher opens a Browse dialog box—similar to the one File Manager opens. Figure 6.5 shows this dialog box pointing to the LView file. Double-click the file lview1b.exe, and WSGopher adds it to the list of viewers. The next time it retrieves a JPEG file, WSGopher will launch LView to display it.

This dialog box lets you search your hard drive for viewers for all file extensions. When you find the application on your hard drive, select it and click OK, or double-click its .exe file. The Browse dialog box will close. Click the Add button.

Fig. 6.5

The name of this Browse dialog box changes depending on what extension you enter in the File Extension text box.

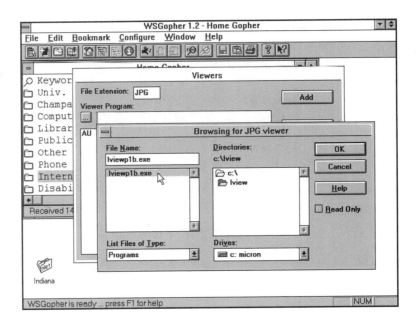

WSGopher will then add the extension and path to its associated application to the Viewers dialog box. The next time WSGopher retrieves a file with this extension, it will launch the application you defined here, rather than use any File Manager association for that file type.

The large text box in the Viewers dialog box lists all the file types you've defined applications for with this dialog box. You can change the association for an extension or delete it altogether.

(!)(Tip)

> You don't define every file type for every viewer in this dialog box. If there is not an association defined here, WSGopher checks File Manager. If a viewer is not set up in either place, WSGopher lets you know it can't display the file. Then it's up to you to define a viewer.

How many viewers you set up and how much time you spend tweaking them will depend on your usage habits. A lot of the files in Gopherspace are text, and WSGopher handles them itself. Other popular file types are GIFs and JPEGs for images, and it's easy to set up a program that will display them. Software applications that you retrieve with WSGopher just get written to your PC's hard drive.

Those three file types—text, images, and software—comprise a lot of what's out there, but you'll be able to deal with other file types as you encounter them.

Setting up a Telnet program

The other types of helper applications we talked about are Telnet and TN/3270 applications. Remember Telnet? It's a way to log into a remote computer as a terminal. The Telnet files you find in Gopherspace are really Telnet connection files.

When you select one of these files with WSGopher, WSGopher gives the connection information to your Telnet application. First, of course, WSGopher needs to know where your Telnet program is. You tell WSGopher where your Telnet application is through the Configure menu:

1 Launch WSGopher. You don't need to be online.

2 Choose Configure, Telnet/3270 Path. The Edit Path dialog box appears, as shown in figure 6.6.

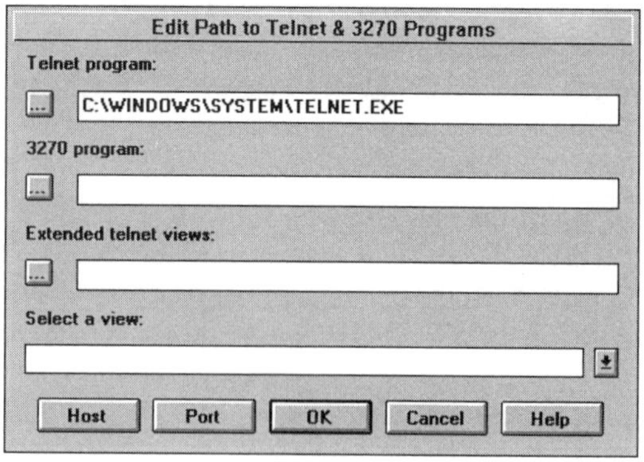

Fig. 6.6
The most important line in this dialog box is the first one. Add the path to your Telnet application here.

Edit Path to Telnet & 3270 Programs
Telnet program:
[...] C:\WINDOWS\SYSTEM\TELNET.EXE
3270 program:
[...]
Extended telnet views:
[...]
Select a view:
[ ] ±
[Host] [Port] [OK] [Cancel] [Help]

3 Enter the path to the Telnet application or click the Browse button to find the application through the Browsing For Telnet Program dialog box.

4 Click OK after the paths are defined.

After WSGopher knows where your Telnet application is, it will fire it up to make the connection. You may need to see the documentation for that program to edit the command line properly for your Telnet application. The traditional format for the command line is program-name host port. If this is the case with your Telnet program, then you don't need to do anything else. WSGopher will pass the information to the Telnet program.

If you need to edit the Telnet command line, then use the Host and Port buttons to add them after the program's path. For example, if your Telnet program needs to be configured like this:

> Program Host:port. (Note the colon between host and port.)

Then you would enter the path to the program, click the Host button, type **a:**, and click the Port button.

The WSGopher Help system provides more information about Telnet command lines.

What's the difference between Telnet and TN/3270?

Telnet is the Internet standard for remote login. It allows your PC to access remote computers through an Internet connection.

TN/3270 is a special type of Telnet that allows your PC to act like an IBM 3270 terminal after it logs in to the remote connection. We won't go into the intricacies of IBM 3270 terminals here. Suffice it to say that IBM did things a little differently, and so to log in to some IBM mainframes, you need to run this special version of Telnet. You might get a TN/3270 program from your Internet Service Provider, although not all providers include one with their software.

Where to find Gopher's friends

You'll find helper applications in many places—on the Net, on the shelf of a local computer store, and maybe even on your computer.

 (Tip)

> WSGopher installs with a couple of bookmark categories labeled Software. These might be good places to start looking.

Programs you might have

Some potential viewers may be software you already have—things that are part of the Windows operating system or that came installed on your computer. Do you already have these programs?

- Mplayer is short for Media Player, a program for playing sound and video files.

- Windows Telnet is a Telnet application that comes with the network versions of Windows 3.11.

- Soundo'LE is the sound player that comes with the Soundblaster sound card.

If you have a multimedia PC, you may have other sound and video players installed. If you have an account with an Internet Service Provider, they may have given you a Telnet application with your service account.

File archives

Of course, the Internet is renowned as a place to find software. Any Gopher site can contain all kinds of Gopher items. However, you will also find sites that specialize in one type of file or another. You can find these archives through the list of Gopher sites in Chapter 14 of this book. You may also run into them while simply prowling around the Net with WSGopher. Here are some things to look for:

- LView is an image viewer that will handle most formats of graphics you'll find in Gopherspace, most importantly, GIFs and JPEGs.

- WinGIF is a shareware GIF viewer.

- MPEGPLAY is a player for MPEG video files. It requires that you use Win32s if you're running Windows instead of Windows NT.

- NCSA Telnet is just like it sounds—a Telnet application from NCSA at the University of Illinois.

Some Gopher sites keep large directories of certain types of files. You'll find software archives that let you retrieve binary files, or more likely, ZIP files of software programs. Some sites archive sound or video files, and many places on the Net keep directories of image files. After you find a site you want to get back to, save the bookmark so that WSGopher can fetch it again.

Here are a couple of FTP archives you can gopher to. Use the File, New Gopher Item command to connect to these addresses. See Chapter 14, "Listing of Gopher Sites," for a few others.

- **gopher.cica.indiana.edu**

- **sunsite.unc.edu**

Software you can buy

There are commercial software programs that you can use with WSGopher. With commercial software, you usually get a support contact and some form of documentation. Here are a couple of programs you may want to purchase:

- PaintShop Pro is an image viewer that will display most any graphics file you find.

- NetManage Telnet is the Telnet application that comes with NetManage's Chameleon TCP/IP software. You may purchase it yourself, or it may come as part of your Internet Service Provider's software.

Telneting to libraries

There are lots of computers on the Internet that you can Telnet to—too many to begin counting. Of all of these potential Telnet sites, the ones you may use most with Gopher are **libraries**. As the Internet has grown in the last 5 to 10 years, libraries around the world have taken advantage of the Internet to share information about their collections.

Many university libraries make their card catalogs and other services available through Telnet connections. Gopher provides a great way to discover those connections and hook up to them via a Gopher Telnet item.

As with many Gopher journeys, start at the University of Minnesota or the WSGopher bookmarks to find connections to libraries all over the world.

Other Gopher Activities

The everyday details of WSGopher, like its print, save, and copy features, are part of what makes it an easy tool to use.

Accessing the Internet is all about getting to files and information that are online. After you find that information, you may want to bring it back to your PC.

You'll want to save some of the files you find for future reference, or copy parts of them into your own documents. You may find it easier to read a printed text file than to scroll through it on your PC's monitor. And by using default retrieval directories, WSGopher makes it easy for you to keep track of whatever you find while cruising online.

Like all good tools, WSGopher helps you accomplish the major task at hand, but also does a good job with the details as well. This chapter explains some of the more day-to-day things that WSGopher does, other than cruising the Internet. It explains things like saving and printing, and where WSGopher puts files that it retrieves.

Where does WSGopher file your information?

While you're searching Gopherspace, WSGopher will occasionally write files to your hard drive. When you retrieve a file, like a graphic, WSGopher copies the file to the hard drive so that it can hand it off to a helper application. Sometimes you'll want WSGopher to save a text file. Sometimes WSGopher just needs to create a temporary file. Before you let WSGopher start saving files all over your hard drive, let's take a minute to see where WSGopher will be putting things.

Unless you tell it otherwise, WSGopher will copy files to your Temp directory, if the TEMP environment variable is set. If your system doesn't have a temp directory, WSGopher will use the directory where it's installed, probably c:\wsgopher.

?Q&A

I don't know if I have a TEMP environment variable set. How can I tell?

If you're not sure that you have temp directory, first check in the Windows File Manager to see if there's a directory on your hard drive named TEMP. Then check your AUTOEXEC.BAT file to see if it contains a line that looks like this;

```
SET TEMP=C:\WINDOWS\TEMP
```

The Temp directory may be in your Windows directory, or anywhere else on your hard drive. If it's not there, you can add this line to your AUTOEXEC.BAT file, but be careful. If you're not sure how to edit the AUTOEXEC.BAT file, DON'T. This file controls the way your computer starts up. Check the DOS documentation if you've never edited this file before.

To set a specific directory to save WSGopher files in, open the Gopher Directories dialog box:

1 Choose <u>C</u>onfigure, Local <u>D</u>irectories.

The Gopher Directories dialog box opens, as shown in figure 7.1.

Now, simply enter the paths for the directories where you want WSGopher to save files.

Fig. 7.1
This dialog box has sample paths for the WSGopher default directories. You can point them to any directory you choose.

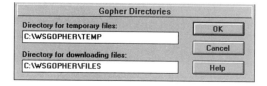

2 Enter the path where you want WSGopher to write temporary files.

3 Enter the path where you want WSGopher to write downloaded files.

4 Click OK to save these settings, or Cancel to close without saving.

Both paths may point to the same directory, and WSGopher will still delete or save the proper files. Even though you define these default directories, you can get WSGopher to copy files in other directories as well.

How to save and delete the files you retrieve

Though WSGopher will retrieve many types of files, for the purpose of this section, let's split them into two types:

- Text files

- Images, video, sound, and binary files

WSGopher saves text files slightly differently from graphics, video, or zip files. These next two sections will look at how WSGopher saves text and other types of files, and how you can tell WSGopher to delete files when you close it. First let's look at text files.

Saving a text file

Many of the items you'll find in Gopherspace are text files. When you retrieve a text file, WSGopher always displays it in a WSGopher text window. You can read the file immediately or later.

If you save the location of a text file with a bookmark, you can always get back to it easily. However, sometimes, for some very good reasons, it's just more convenient to have a copy of the file on your own computer. By saving a file to your hard drive you can:

- Read the file later, without using up valuable online time.

- Refer back to the file quickly without having to get back online.

Because text files appear in a WSGopher window, you can save them onto your computer easily. After WSGopher retrieves a text file and displays it in a text window:

1 Select File, Save Item. The Save Gopher Text File As dialog box appears, as shown in figure 7.2.

2 Check the drive and directory where you want to save the file.

3 Click OK, to save the file, or click Cancel to close the dialog box without saving the file.

(!) (Tip)

When WSGopher saves things, it first checks to see if you defined a default directory. Then it checks for your PC's Temp directory. If neither of those two are there, it defaults to the directory where it is installed.

In the Save Gopher Text File As dialog box, WSGopher creates a filename based on the item's name, with a default extension, .txt. However, you can select any filename, directory, and extension you want. If you go ahead and save the file, the status line of the text file window reminds you where you saved it, as shown in figure 7.3

Fig. 7.2
Use this dialog box to save the file wherever you want on your hard drive.

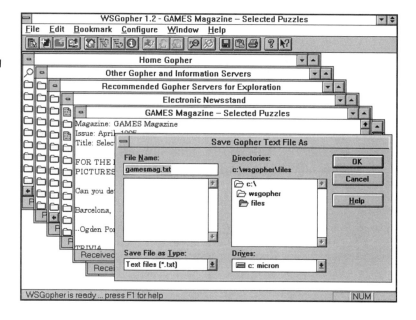

Fig. 7.3
Did you save that file without noting the directory it was going into? Just watch the status line.

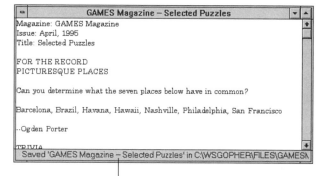

The status line always tells you where WSGopher saved the file

Saving a non-text file

When WSGopher retrieves files other than text—like a full-color national weather map, or new game software—it writes those files to your PC's hard drive. Depending on how you have WSGopher set up, it will prompt you for a file name and directory, or it will use a default file name and directory.

When you double-click an image file, for example. WSGopher will open a Select Gopher File for Download dialog box. This dialog box displays the default name WSGopher gave the file and lets you choose a directory on your hard drive to save it. Except for its title, this dialog box looks exactly like the Save Gopher Text File As dialog box shown in figure 7.2. Click OK to go ahead with the download, or Cancel to forget it.

Unless you tell it otherwise, WSGopher retrieves these files to the directory for downloading files that you assign through Configure, Local Directories. WSGopher will delete these files when you close the application. However, while WSGopher is retrieving a file, you can tell it to save that file for later use, in the download window.

Figure 7.4 shows WSGopher retrieving a GIF image file. To tell WSGopher to save this file, you would check the box next to Save File For Later Use. WSGopher will save the file to the same directory, but it won't delete the file when you shut down WSGopher.

Fig. 7.4

The checkboxes give you the option to view the file now or save it for later. By saving the file for later use, you are telling WSGopher not to delete the file when you quit.

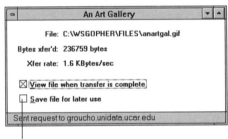

Click here to save the file

How WSGopher names a file

WSGopher creates a filename by shortening the name of the Gopher item to eight characters and adding an appropriate extension. So if you stumble across a GIF file called A Wine Bottle with Mona Lisa, WSGopher will supply a filename of awinebot.gif.

Once again, this is a default, chosen for your convenience. If you want to name a text file

something else, like monalisa.gif, you can do that in the Save Gopher Text File As dialog box. You can rename other types of files in the Select File For Gopher Download dialog box, if you have WSGopher set to show that each time you retrieve a file. You can also rename files through the Windows File Manager after WSGopher retrieves them.

⊗<Caution>

Don't try to save everything you retrieve. While the files on the Internet are seemingly infinite, your hard drive is not. After you spend several sessions on the Internet, you may find you have to throw away files you thought you wanted to keep, just to make room for more.

It's like renting videos. You may rent a lot of videos that you like, but you probably don't want to own a copy of every one. Where would you keep all the tapes? Sometimes though, you find one you really do want to own, because you really like it or its very useful, and you buy the tape. In the case of the Internet, you just save the file to your hard drive.

⊘Q&A

I don't want to see the Select Gopher File for Download dialog box every time WSGopher retrieves a file. How do I control that?

You can set WSGopher to simply retrieve files with default names into the default directory, without viewing the Select Gopher File for Download dialog box every time. To make WSGopher work this way, choose Configure, User Options. Then check the box next to Use The Generated Filename, Check For Uniqueness, Don't Prompt Me. When this option is set, WSGopher will simply save files to your default download directory.

Deleting a file

After a long night's session online you might not remember which files you told WSGopher to save after you shut down. You might also just want to look at the files you've retrieved so far with WSGopher. And if you've been packing your hard drive with sound and videos files, you might even have to delete some files just so you have room to download more.

 Plain English, please!

A **session** is the period of time you spend running WSGopher, from when you open the application, until you shut it down. You don't need to be online the whole time. You can manage bookmarks or check the status of downloaded files while you're offline. **99**

In any case, let's take a look at WSGopher's Downloaded Files dialog box, shown in figure 7.5. To bring up this dialog box, choose <u>F</u>ile, <u>D</u>elete Files.

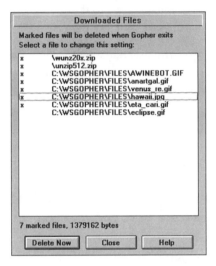

The main box in this dialog box lists all the files WSGopher has retrieved for you during this session. Those files with an x next to them are marked for deletion. The line below the list of files shows you the total size and number of files WSGopher will delete when you shut it down.

Clicking any item in the list toggles it to be saved or deleted. To tell WSGopher not to delete a file, click on the file to unmark it. If a file is not marked, click on it and an x will appear beside it.

To delete files right now, mark the files you want to delete and click Delete Now. WSGopher will delete the files and close the Downloaded Files dialog box. This will free up valuable hard disk space and let you continue searching Gopherspace for more files.

You can print from WSGopher

With WSGopher you can print Gopher directories and text files, assuming, of course, that there's a printer hooked to your PC. You can also preview a page before you print to see what it will look like. The Print Setup and Page Setup commands let you configure your printer and choose the page layout for files WSGopher prints.

To print with WSGopher, make the directory or text file that you want to print the active window and choose File, Print. The WSGopher Print dialog box appears, shown in figure 7.6. From this dialog box, check the settings and click OK to print.

Fig. 7.6

The WSGopher print dialog box. This dialog box may look different depending on what version of Windows your PC runs.

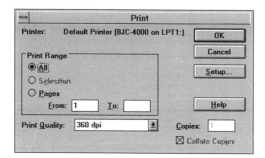

With the WSGopher Print dialog box you can print all of the document or only certain pages. If you selected text in the WSGopher window before choosing Print, then you can print only that selected text.

Page Preview

If you want to see what a document will look like on the printed page, before you print it, choose File, Print Preview. WSGopher displays the document in Print Preview mode, as shown in figure 7.7. This feature works like print preview in many word processing programs.

From the Print Preview window, you can get an idea of what the page will look like when printed. WSGopher opens the file so you can see the whole page, though it's not quite readable. You can scroll through the document, zoom in and out, and print the document with the buttons at the top of the window. The following table describes the Print Preview buttons:

Button	What it does
Print	Closes the preview window and opens the WSGopher Print dialog box
Next Page	Scrolls to the next page in the document
Prev Page	Scrolls to the previous page in the document
Two Page	Displays two pages, side by side
Zoom In	Zooms in to display the document in larger type
Zoom Out	Zooms out to display the document in smaller type
Close	Closes the print preview window and returns you to WSGopher

Fig. 7.7
Check the layout of a document before you print. Maybe a different font or margin will display the file better.

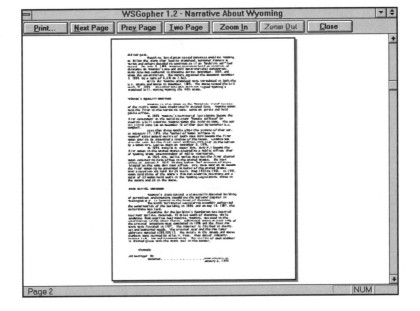

Print Setup

WSGopher's Print Setup dialog box lets you select a printer, a page orientation, and a paper size and source (see fig. 7.8). From this dialog box you can also control more detailed printer specific settings with the Options button.

To open the Print Setup dialog box, choose File, Print Setup.

Fig. 7.8

The settings in this dialog box will vary depending on your printer.

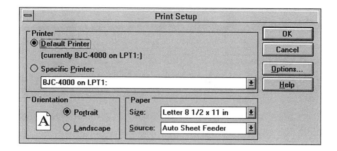

Page Setup

The Printed Page Setup dialog box, shown in Figure 7.9, lets you control the look of pages you print with your WSGopher documents. To open this dialog box, choose File, Page Setup.

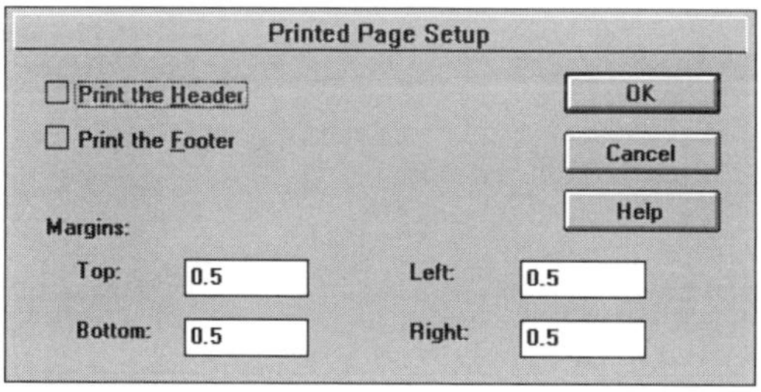

Fig. 7.9

Change the margins, and add headers and footers with this dialog box; then preview those changes by viewing a text file with the Print Preview dialog box.

From this dialog box, you set WSGopher to print headers and footers for the documents you print. To set either of these options to *on*, click in the checkbox beside them.

At the top of each page, WSGopher prints a header: the title of the document with a line under it. At the bottom of each page, WSGopher prints a footer: *Page* and the page number with a line separating the text from the page number.

The margins control the amount of white space surrounding the text. Enter fractions as decimals—for example, three quarters of an inch equals .75".

Click OK to close the dialog box and save your changes, or Cancel to close without saving any changes.

Copy text to the Clipboard

Would you like to quote text from a Gopher file in a report that you're writing? Maybe you'd like to list the contents of a particular Gopher site in a memo to encourage people to go there. WSGopher will copy directory entries or text files to the Windows clipboard. You can then paste this text into whatever other applications you want. Copying text with WSGopher follows two simple rules:

- In a directory, WSGopher copies the entire contents of the window.

- In a text file, if you select text, then WSGopher copies only that text; if no text is selected, then it copies the entire file.

There are three ways to copy something from a WSGopher Window:

- Choose <u>E</u>dit, <u>C</u>opy

- Click the Clipboard button

- Press Ctrl+C

After you copy to the Clipboard, the status bar at the bottom of the directory or text window tells you the amount of text copied. The status bar, shown in figure 7.10, gives you an idea of how much you just copied.

Fig. 7.10
Don't leave a lot of text in the Clipboard for long. Paste it into a document and save it or you'll forget it's there and accidentally copy over it.

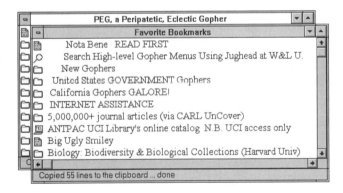

> **①(Tip)**
>
> Anytime you copy something to the Clipboard, you overwrite what was there. After you copy something, be sure you paste it into another document before you forget and copy over it.

Change the fonts

WSGopher lets you control the fonts it uses to display item descriptions and file text. You can set these fonts to make WSGopher look the way you want and change the size of the fonts so that you can read them easily on your PC's monitor. WSGopher will also let you specify a font to use when printing documents instead of printing files with the display font.

Display fonts

To change the fonts WSGopher uses to display directories and text, choose Configure, Fonts. Figure 7.11 shows the sub-menu under Fonts.

Fig. 7.11
Want to change the look of your WSGopher display? Choose distinct fonts for text and directory listings.

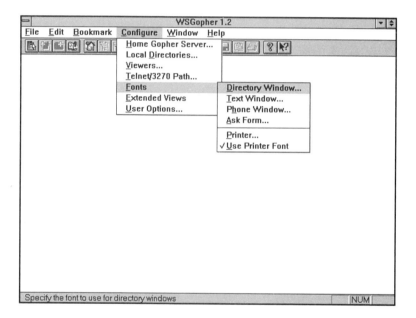

The way you change the fonts for any of these parts of WSGopher is pretty much the same. For example, let's change the font that WSGopher uses to list items in directory windows. Choose Configure, Fonts, Directory Window. The dialog box shown in figure 7.12 opens.

Fig. 7.12
This dialog box lists the fonts available on your PC, which may vary from the list you see here.

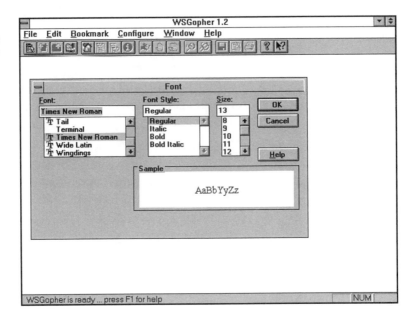

From this dialog box you can choose a font from the Font list at the left. Then set a style, like Bold or Italic, from the Font Style list, and finally a size from the Size list. An example of the settings you make will appear in the Sample area. Choose OK to apply your changes and close this dialog box, or Cancel to close the dialog box without making any changes.

(Tip)

Because text in Gopher files is usually formatted with spaces instead of tabs and tables, you may want to use a proportional font like Courier to display files with information in columns.

WSGopher will change the font in all open windows of the kind you edited. So if you change the Directory Font and there are four directory windows open, it will change the font of all four.

Also, WSGopher doesn't change the size of the window when you change the font. If you change the size of the text, or simply choose a font that displays differently, scroll bars may appear or disappear as needed.

Take some time and choose a font that displays well on your monitor, and that you think looks good. Different users have different tastes, and WSGopher lets you choose the look you want.

Printer Fonts

WSGopher will pick from one of two fonts when it prints a directory or text file. It will print one of these ways:

- With the same font as the window being printed from

- With a font you select for your printer through the Font dialog box

To set which preference WSGopher will use, choose Configure, Fonts. See the sub-menu item Use Printer Font. If this menu item has a check mark by it then all printing will use the font you defined in the Font dialog box. Otherwise, the WSGopher will print using the window font, or one close to it.

To change this setting, select Use Printer Font from the sub-menu. This removes the check mark if it wasn't there, or adds it if it was.

?Q&A

The font I chose didn't print very well. Why?

Depending on the printer and resolution you use, some fonts may look better than others after you print them. Or you may like to use a screen font (for text files or directories) that for some reason doesn't print very well. It may not be installed on your printer and therefore the printer is trying to approximate the font you asked it for.

The WSGopher option Use Printer Font lets you select a different font for printing that looks good without having to change your display font.

Part III:

Finding What You Want with Gopher

Searching with Jughead

In this chapter:

- What's Jughead?
- Finding Jughead on Gopher menus
- Search a Gopher with Jughead
- How to find information with Jughead

That information was somewhere on this Gopher, but now you can't find it? Relax—no need to search every menu; Jughead will find it.

It could happen to you. You visit a Gopher and find an interesting piece of information. Maybe you found an online poetry collection or a copy of the U.S. Federal budget. Later you want to view that information again, but you can't remember the menu where you found it. Wouldn't it be nice to have an assistant you could ask, "I know I found that thing on this Gopher—where *was* that, anyway?" Jughead can be that assistant. Jughead is a search service that you find on a lot of Gophers.

Did you say Jughead?

It might be difficult to have a lot of confidence in a piece of software called Jughead if you don't know anything about it. But in spite of the name, after you get to know this handy tool better, Jughead can become one of your favorite helpers.

The origins of Jughead

A nice thing about the Internet is that a lot of its software is written by people who just want to solve a particular problem. A lot of times, they make their software available for free to people on the Internet who need to solve the same problem. This is the case with Jughead. Jughead was written by Rhett "Jonzy" Jones at the University of Utah. The software lets you look for menu items on your favorite Gopher, based on one or more words from the item's title.

 Plain English, please!

Because Gopher is organized as a collection of menus, here we refer to a line from a Gopher menu as a **menu item**. In WSGopher, each item is shown with an icon on the left which tells you what kind of item it is; it might be a file, or a program, or another menu level. Each item has a description following the icon which we'll refer to as the item's title. **9 9**

Jughead actually stands for a much longer name: Jonzy's Universal Gopher Hierarchy Excavation And Display. Why such an odd name? Because it spells JUGHEAD, of course! Jughead was written after two other Internet search programs that you will learn about in the next two chapters—Veronica and Archie—had already been written. Jonzy created another Internet search program and named it after another friend of that red-headed comic book character, Archie.

What Jughead will do for you

Jughead works along with Gopher to keep track of all the menu items on that Gopher. It creates a search index of all the items to make it easier for you to find things.

Plain English, please!

A computer program's **search index** is a lot like a book index. You can look for a word in the index in the back of this book and the index tells you what pages that word can be found on. A computer's search index is similar. You give the program a word and it looks in the index to find where that word occurs; then it shows you the information it finds. An index is different from a bookmark. A bookmark points to only one place, but an index can find information any place within an online collection.

You can use your Gopher program to tell Jughead to look for menus, files, and other Internet services. You might be looking for a menu of Internet library catalogs, a file with information about the Internet, or an Internet BBS system. Jughead prompts you to type in one or more words, and lets you use commands to narrow the scope of the search.

Jughead makes it easier to find a menu item that is particularly hard to find. For instance, most Gophers have a lot of directories, and Jughead can find information that may be buried several layers deep on a Gopher site. It can also display a group of related menu items that it gathers from different places within the Gopher menu structure.

It's not always easy to find Jughead

Jughead is installed on a lot of Gopher sites, but unfortunately, not on all of them. Most of the time, Jughead is identified by name, but sometimes it's hidden behind a more generic menu title.

Because Jughead was created to find things on one particular Gopher server, as opposed to all of Gopherspace, you can usually find it near the top level of a Gopher system's menus. The person that runs a particular Gopher server decides where to put Jughead. Many times it's on the first menu you see. Sometimes it is within a menu like About This Gopher; or it could have its own menu.

The Gopher at the University of Utah, where Jughead was created, has a list of some of the places where Jughead is available. You'll find that list, called All Known Jughead Servers, at **gopher.utah.edu** in the Search Menu Titles Using Jughead menu. From your Home Gopher, you'll need to open a New Gopher item and open **gopher.utah.edu**.

There is also a Search Other Institutions Using Jughead menu, which lets you use Jughead on many of those same servers. You can see what this looks like in figure 8.1. If the Gopher you usually use doesn't have a Jughead search service installed, the Utah menu is a good place to go to experiment with using Jughead.

Fig. 8.1
The Jughead menu at the University of Utah has a nice collection of Jughead examples.

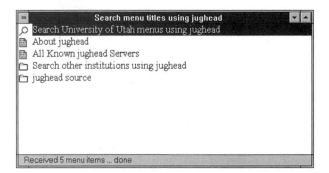

How do you know it's Jughead?

The one thing that most Jughead menu items have in common is that they are named something like Search this Gopher... But they might not always include the words ...with Jughead. For example, to give you some idea of what a Jughead menu item might look like, we've provided some actual Jughead search items from Gopher menus on the Internet:

- Search Gopher Titles at the University of Minnesota

- Search University of Utah Menus Using Jughead

- Search Menu Titles of UNT Gopher by Keyword

- Search This Gopher

- Search UNC-CH Gopherspace with Jughead (via SunSITE)

As you can see, the only thing that these items have in common is that they all include the word Search and they refer to one particular Gopher server.

 Q&A

> ### I've found something but I'm not sure it's Jughead. Is there any way to tell?
>
> The way you can tell you've found Jughead is by asking its version number. In WSGopher, double-click on the item to bring up the search box, type **?version**, and press Enter or click on the search button. If it's Jughead, it comes back with a message like, "This version of Jughead is 1.0.4." If you don't get that message, then that search is most likely not Jughead.

Finding information and resources with Jughead

Jughead is pretty easy to use. To search with Jughead, all you need to know is what you want to find. Jughead tries to match your search words with the words that are part of Gopher item titles. If you use the search term Document, you'll probably find files you can read. If you search for Software, you might find software archives. You can also think about searching for a particular topic. You might want to find information about electronic mail, so you could search for Mail.

Basic searching

The easiest way to learn is by doing, so… If you've got WSGopher handy, you can follow along. First, we need a Gopher to search, and the Library of Congress provides an interesting target. To open a new Gopher in WSGopher:

1 Choose File, New Gopher Item.

2 In the Title box, type **Library of Congress Gopher** (see fig. 8.2).

3 In the Server Name box, type **marvel.loc.gov**.

4 Click OK.

> The Title box is for information purposes only. If you leave this field blank when opening a new Gopher, you will still be able to get to the site—it just won't be titled.

Fig. 8.2
You can use the Fetch this Gopher Item dialog box to visit interesting servers like the Library of Congress Gopher.

After you are connected to the Library of Congress Gopher by following the preceding steps, you'll see its top level (or root) menu. Next, find Jughead by selecting the menu entitled, Search LC Marvel Menus. This search menu is the last item on the root menu. Double-click on Search LC Marvel Menus and you see a menu like the one in figure 8.3.

Fig. 8.3
The Search LC Marvel Menus menu includes a Jughead search which you can use to find a lot of information.

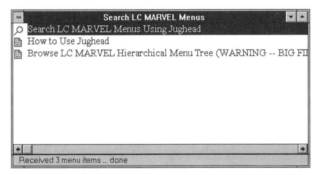

If you click on Search LC Marvel Menus Using Jughead, a search box appears on your screen (see fig. 8.4). You can type your search word into the box and press Enter, or click the Search button. Let's try searching for the word **music** and see what we get.

Fig. 8.4

A Jughead search for music yields a list of 123 items.

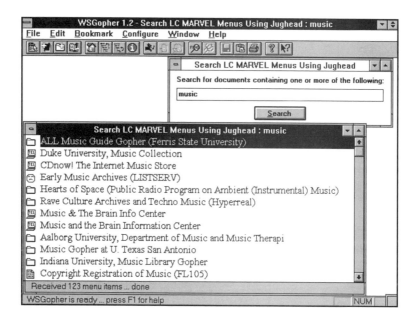

This search finds over 100 entries within the Marvel menus. Some of the items are files and some are other directories. This is quite a long list, but you can limit your search even further.

Let's suppose you are just interested in folk music. You back up one menu item to the search box, but this time type in the words **folk** and **music**. This shortens the resulting list considerably (see fig. 8.5).

Fig 8.5

Limiting the search shortens the list to 12 items.

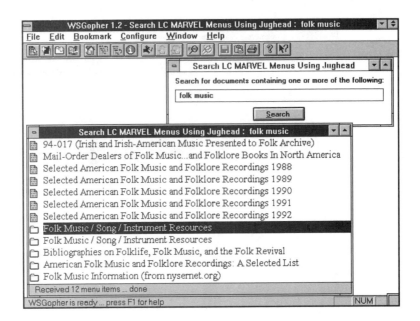

Using the asterisk to control your search

Let's explore another possibility for our search. Suppose that you want to find music libraries listed within the Marvel Gopher. You would need some way to find both library and libraries because both the singular and the plural are used in the library names.

Instead of looking for music library you could look for **music librar***. This example finds all items which contain the word music together with the words library, libraries, librarians, and so on (see fig. 8.6). The asterisk (*), which is often called a wild card, matches any characters that occur after the first part of the word.

Fig. 8.6
An asterisk can help you narrow your search, like when you are just looking for music libraries.

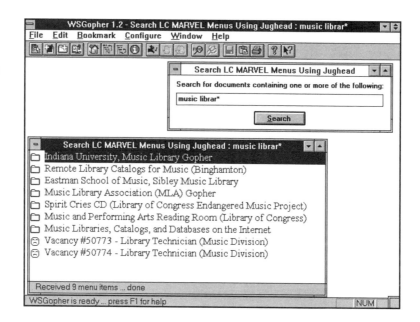

⊗ <Caution> An asterisk should appear at the end of a word fragment. Any characters to the immediate right of the asterisk will be ignored. For example, librar*s matches the same words as librar*—the s has no effect in the search.

More search possibilities

If you search for music library, Jughead shows you an item only if both music AND library are found in its title. Sometimes, however, you might want to expand your search and find items that have music OR jazz in their title. The words AND, OR, and NOT can be used within your search to exert this kind of control. For example:

- **cats AND dogs**—Finds item titles that contain both the words cats and dogs

- **fish OR bait**—Finds item titles that contain either fish or bait

- **water NOT oil**—Finds item titles that contain water but excludes them if they contain oil

Let's suppose you want to find information on music, including jazz but excluding folk music. In the search field, type **music or jazz not folk** to get such a result (see fig. 8.7).

Fig. 8.7
You can customize your search by using the words and, or, and not, such as when you want to find references to jazz and other music, but not folk music.

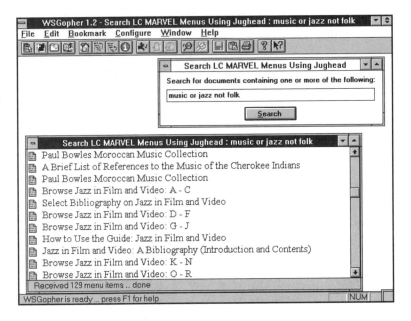

 You can mix AND, OR, and NOT any way you want in your search, but you should avoid making your search too complex. It will just take longer and might not find much information.

Special commands

Jughead has some special commands that you can use to get more information about Jughead and to control the number of items that are displayed. They all start with a question mark and are used as the first part of a search. The five commands are as follows:

- **?help**—Tells Jughead to show you its online help file

- **?version**—Let's you find out what Jughead version you are using

- **?all**—Returns all possible matched menu items

- **?limit=#**—Limits the number of matched items to a designated number (#). For instance, if you wanted to only see the first ten items found, you would type **?limit=10** before your search phrase.

- **?range=#-#**—Only returns a range of the matched search items. For example, if you knew that what you were looking for was far down on a list, you might ask Jughead to show you only items 50-75 by typing in **?range=50-75** before your search phrase.

The three commands that control the number of items shown from the search, ?all, ?limit, and ?range, are always followed by search words. The ?help and ?version commands can optionally be followed by search words. The help file or version message item will appear as the first entries in the search results (see fig. 8.8).

Fig. 8.8

Combining a search with the ?help command not only finds jazz items, but also returns a Jughead Help document that you can browse.

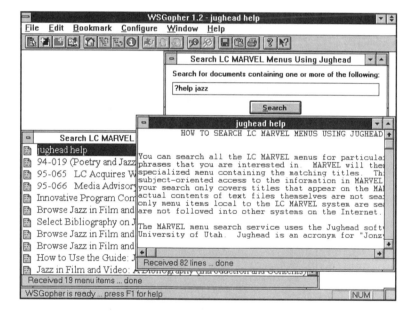

You might be wondering why you need the ?all command. Jughead only shows you the first 1,024 items from a search unless you use ?all or use ?limit with a number greater than 1,024. Granted, you may rarely want or need to look at that many items from a search, but it's a handy fact to know when you do.

The ?range command is useful when you know there's a long list of items that can be found by a search, but you only want to look at 10 or 20 at a time. The advantage is that 10 or 20 items will be displayed on your screen a lot faster than 1,000. Figure 8.9 shows an example.

Fig. 8.9

Displaying a range lets you browse some voluminous search output a few items at a time.

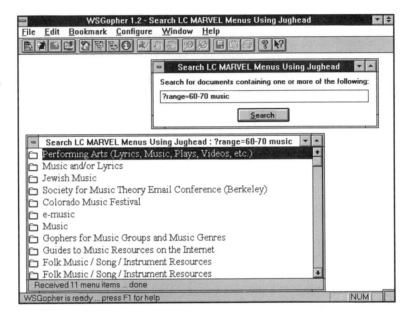

Searching with Veronica

In this chapter:

- What is Veronica?

- What can I find with Veronica?

- Using Veronica to discover information on Gopher

- Finding Veronica servers on the Internet

So many Gopher sites and so much information, how will you ever find what you need? Call Veronica.

Imagine that you're in a big library looking for all the books you can find about elephants. In this library, books on different topics are scattered across different floors . To make things worse, the organization of each floor is slightly different from all the others. One way to find books about elephants would be to visit each floor and walk up and down each aisle, gradually collecting all the books on elephants you could find. It would take a long time to find them, especially in a library with thousands of floors. It would be quicker if you had a catalog to tell you where those books were located, and a helper to run and bring them all to you.

Gopherspace is like that library. Each individual Gopher server is like a different floor, with each one organized a little differently from the others. To find a particular piece of information on Gopher, you can visit each Gopher server and look in all the menus until you find what you are looking for, but that could take a lifetime.

That's where Veronica comes in. Veronica is like a helper who will find out where things are located and then go and get them for you to look at. Veronica can do this because it knows what information is available on each

Gopher server in the world. Veronica can quickly search all the Gopher servers for you and find the specific kinds of information that you ask for, even information about elephants. With such power and knowledge, Veronica is definitely worth getting to know.

What is Veronica and how does it work?

Veronica is a kind of Internet server that finds information on particular topics on Gopher servers throughout the world and then lets you access that information. (The name Veronica officially stands for Very Easy Rodent-Oriented Net-wide Index to Computerized Archives.) You can search Veronica for a particular item by using your WSGopher client program.

Plain English, please!

A **server** is a program that works behind the scenes to gather and transmit information. An Internet server program can run on a computer that's in the next room or halfway around the world. A **client program** is the go-between that sends your requests to the server and then shows you the results on your own computer.

Veronica regularly reads Gopher menus from around the world and maintains an index of over 15 million items found on those Gophers. It's like having a giant card catalog for all of Gopherspace. Veronica's index lets you search for Gopher items in a number of different ways. Just like a card catalog lets you search for a book by its title, author, or subject, so too does Veronica allow you to find information in different ways. Items in Veronica's index get updated about once a month.

Because the indexing and searching process can take quite a lot of a computer's time and storage space, Veronica servers are not nearly as common as Gopher servers. Some sites on the Internet provide Veronica as a public service. Other sites provide Veronica only for their subscribers or local users.

Veronica can help you find many different kinds of information and services. Veronica lets you do a keyword search of items from Gopher menus. It can return all types of items or just one type of Gopher item. Because Gopher can bring together all kinds of items, you might end up searching for programs that can be downloaded through Gopher, or you might find a UseNet news post about a topic that interests you. For instance, if you searched for the word **chess**, you might find some shareware chess programs ready to download, or you could find news message files with questions and answers about chess.

❝ *Plain English, please!*

A **keyword search** matches significant subject words with words in a computerized index. Some of the unimportant words that aren't put in the computer index are: the, a, to, and or. ❞

Using Veronica is no more difficult than using your WSGopher client program. After you find a Veronica search item, you select it from the menu and type in one or more words to search for. You can also use commands that control how the search is done. After you enter the search information, your Gopher client contacts the Veronica server and Veronica sends back a menu of Gopher items that match your search criteria.

Let's say, for example, you want to find as many Internet phone books as possible from sites around the world. You can search for the word phone and limit the search type to phone book servers. If you're looking for an online picture of an eagle, you can search for eagle and limit the scope of your search to GIF and other image types. As you can see, Veronica can be a great help in reducing all that Gopher-based Internet information into usable chunks that are customized to your needs.

❶(Tip)

> Veronica and Jughead are similar because they can both search for items found on Gopher menus. The difference, however, is that Jughead can only search one particular Gopher server while Veronica can search all the Gopher servers in the world.

A Veronica search of Gopherspace

If you start from WSGopher's Home server at the University of Illinois, it's easy to find Veronica (see fig. 9.1):

1 Double-click on the Other Gopher and Information Servers menu.

2 From the next menu, double-click Search titles in Gopherspace Using Veronica.

3 To get the search started, double-click on Find Gopher Directories by Title word(s) (via NYSERNet).

Fig. 9.1
You can find a Veronica search on WSGopher's Home server at the University of Illinois.

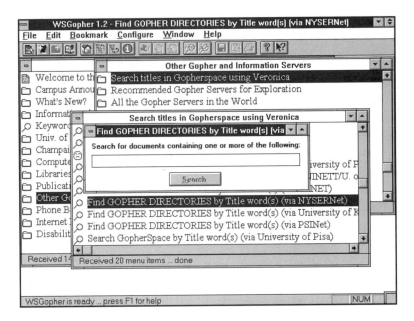

As you can see, if you open a Veronica search from the menu in WSGopher, a box pops up with a blank line and a Search button. When faced with a blank search request, you only need to type a word or several words that might appear in the title of some Gopher servers.

To try Veronica, let's search for food. Perhaps a good recipe for pasta is in order; so from the Find Gopher Directories by Title word(s) (via NYSERNet), you would:

1 Type the word **pasta**.

2 Press Enter or click the Search button.

The result may be several pages of pasta recipes as you can see in figure 9.2.

Fig. 9.2
The search for pasta
returns 120 items
ranging from pasta
recipes to pasta shops.

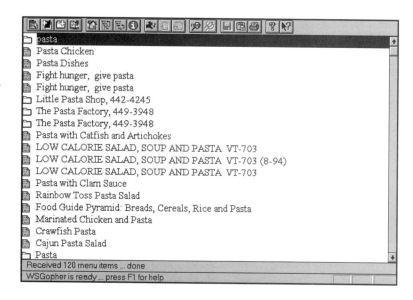

When you submit a Veronica search three results are actually possible:

- WSGopher might open a window containing a one-line message saying that the server is too busy and to try again (as in figure 9.3). If this is the case, close that window to return to the search box, and click the Search button to submit your search again or choose to use a different server.

- You might get a similar message that says no items matched your search. If so, close the window to get back to the search box, and type in a different but similar word and resubmit your search.

- You may find some really neat items. Sweet success!

① (Tip)

Do your Veronica searches when the server is least busy, like late at night, or at midday; or use a server in a place halfway across the world from you where it is already late at night. Another strategy is to pick one Veronica server and repeat your search until it gets processed. (Just close the result window with the sorry message and click again on the Search button.) Sometimes the persistent approach is the best.

Fig. 9.3

A busy Veronica server will only return one item which is actually a message telling you that too many people are trying to do a search.

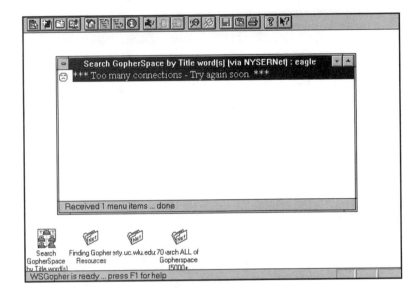

Two words are better than one

When you search all of Gopherspace, it's sometimes surprising how much you can find. One hundred twenty Gopher items are a lot to browse through. Perhaps, you are only interested in pasta salad recipes. You can narrow your search by using **pasta salad** as your search term (see fig. 9.4).

Because we've narrowed the search considerably, you'll notice that the number of items returned is much smaller than in the search for pasta. You find only 15 pasta salad recipes, but you come closer to finding exactly what you're looking for. If you wish, you can look at each one and decide which would be perfect to take to the company picnic.

It is generally a good idea to keep your search terms down to a word or two if at all possible. There may very well be a Gopher item on Classic Ford Mustangs, but what if you happen to search for Ford Classic Cars? They won't match and you'll never know it. A better idea would be to look for Classic Mustangs or Ford Mustangs.

Fig. 9.4
By using two words, you can narrow the scope of your search and find only pasta salad recipes.

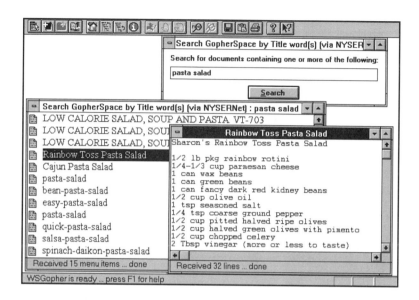

Going wild with wild cards

Suppose that you wanted to look for potato recipes. By default, Veronica exactly matches your search words with the words in Gopher menu items. This means that searching for potato might get you potato pancakes, but it won't get you potatoes au gratin. If you want to find all the possibilities, a wild card is in order. Searching for **potato*** matches potato, potatoe, potatoes, potatoesoup, and so on, as possible keywords (see fig. 9.5).

 Plain English, please!

A **wild card** in a search (represented by an *) can represent anything. The wild card in a Veronica search can match one or many characters. In a search for route, the wild card could represent rs (routers), 66 (route 66) or any other number of terms.

 The asterisk (*) can only be used at the end of a search word and results in a failed search if placed in any other position.

Fig. 9.5

By using a wild card in your search, you can find several variants of a particular word or phrase, like in this case, information about potatoes.

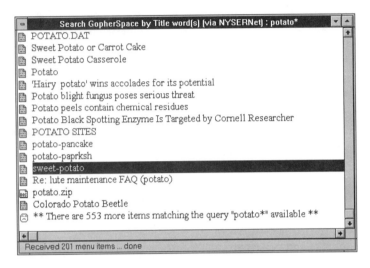

Veronica commands that control your search

In addition to words and wild card combinations, Veronica provides some additional ways to customize and control a search. There are a couple of commands that you might find useful and some other control words that you can use to narrow the scope of the search beyond what a wild card alone can do. There are two commands that you can add to your search words:

- **-m*number*—**Even if there are many possible matches to your search, Veronica only shows you the first 200 items it finds unless you tell it that you want more. The -m command tells Veronica that you want to look at as many items as the *number* that follows it.

- **-t*codes*—**When Veronica is looking for things that match your search, it ordinarily shows you all kinds of Gopher items. It might find files, programs, searches, and many other item types. The -t command, followed by one or more codes representing different Gopher item types, tells Veronica to only look for the kinds of things you need.

In addition to these two commands, there are several more options that you can use to control how your search is done:

- **AND—**If you search for buttons AND bows, Veronica returns an item only if the words buttons and bows are both found

- **OR**—If you search for rain OR snow, Veronica returns an item if either of the words rain or snow is found

- **NOT**—If you include NOT plastic in your search, Veronica will not return an item if the word plastic is found, even if there are other words in the search which are also found.

- **( )**—The parentheses control the order of the search. The items in parentheses are looked for first. For example, if you search for black AND (white OR red), Veronica looks for white or red and if it finds either it will then look for the word black. If it doesn't find white or red, then it will skip that item whether or not it contains the word, black.

Veronica searches don't care whether you use upper- or lowercase letters in your search terms. The order of the search words doesn't matter. In other words, a search for salad pasta finds the same items as one for pasta salad.

Veronica servers also keep a list of stop words. These are words like a, but, on, and so on. These words are so common that they show up in a large number of items. Because they do nothing to narrow your search, Veronica eliminates these common words from the search.

Search commands can appear before or after the search words, but only one command can follow a dash (-). These commands and options are discussed in further detail in the following sections.

Control what Veronica gives you

In the potato example (refer to fig. 9.5), the last item listed indicates that there are 553 more matches on potato than the 200 that Veronica automatically showed you (who knew potatoes were such a hot topic?).

You can tell Veronica you want to see more by using the **-m** command. To find more potato items, specify **potato* -m800** as your search term and you can then browse through the entire list. Asking for 800 items will ensure that you'll see all 753 items (the first 200 plus the remaining 553). You can specify a number that is larger than the number of matches possible and Veronica will just show you as many items as it finds.

(Tip)

If at first you don't find the kind of information you want, try enlarging the search. If it's a popular topic, the item you're looking for might not show up in the first 200 entries. Add the command –m400 to your search words to get back a longer list of possibilities, or add –m800 for an even longer list. Remember, however, that the more items you ask for, the longer it will take Veronica to complete the search.

What Gopher items do you want?

In your search for potato recipes, you might come across items with titles like df940228.jpg Mrs. Potato Head's shocking discovery. This is a picture, not a recipe, and obviously is not what you're looking for. You can probably count on most recipes being text files, so a search of only text files would come closer to meeting your needs.

The -t command controls what type of Gopher items you get. Each item type has its own code. The different kinds of Gopher item codes you can use with the -t command are listed in table 9.1.

Table 9.1 Different types of Gopher item codes used with –t in a search

If you want to find...	Add this command
A plain text file (maybe a pasta recipe)	–t0
A Gopher menu of more items (like a whole bunch of pasta recipes)	–t1
A phone book search (some university campus directories are on Gopher)	–t2
A Macintosh file in BINHEX format (a .hqx file ready to download)	–t4
A binary DOS archive file (.zip and .zoo files, for example)	–t5
A UUEncoded UNIX file (a binary file turned into printable characters)	–t6
A text index search (like Veronica)	–t7
A Telnet session (to use other services like library card catalogs)	–t8
A binary file (like a program or word processor file)	–t9

If you want to find...	Add this command
A GIF image picture file (like a picture of an eagle)	-tg
An HTML file (the kind of files used for World Wide Web)	-tH
Other kinds of image files (like .jpg files)	-tI
An Adobe Portable Document Format (PDF) file (an online document file)	-tP
A digitized sound file (like a CD only a lot smaller)	-ts
A TN3270 session (to use other services on IBM mainframes)	-tT

To find just text files in your potato search, you could use a search word together with the -t command: **potato* -t0** will ask Veronica to find only plain text files about potatoes. You can also search for more than one item type at a time. For example:

- **potato* -t0g**—Finds files about potatoes and GIF image pictures of potatoes

- **potato* -t0lI**—Finds files, directories, and images other than GIF pictures

- **potato* -t0lgI**—Finds files, directories, and all kinds of image files

 **\<Caution\>** There must not be a space between a –t command and any of the item codes. For example, **–tgiP** is the correct command you add to find only GIF images, other images, and PDF files. However, **–t giP** and **–tg i P** are not correct, and will not result in the search that you want.

Doing it the logical way

Veronica supports several elements of a Boolean or, as it's sometimes called, a logical search. The control words AND, OR, and NOT are referred to as Boolean operators and can be used to conduct a more specific search.

Plain English, please!

A **Boolean search** is named after the system of mathematical logic developed by George Boole. Instead of arithmetic operators like plus, minus, divided by, or times, Boolean math uses operators like AND, OR, and NOT (called Boolean operators) to determine a result. Boolean logic is an important concept that controls many computer functions.

By default, if you use two words for your search, Veronica looks for appearances of both in every item. If you look for pasta salad, Veronica would actually look for items containing the words pasta AND salad and return any items for which that condition is true.

To be even more specific, you can use the words OR and NOT to control how Veronica interprets combinations of these words by using parentheses. For example, if you want recipes for pasta salads, sauces, and doughs but you hate spinach, you could use pasta AND (salad OR sauce OR dough) NOT spinach. In this case, Veronica returns combinations of pasta and salad, pasta and sauce, and pasta and dough, but does not show you items that contain the word spinach (see fig. 9.6).

The OR operator is most efficient if it is used in parentheses along with AND or NOT. A search using OR can potentially match a large number of items—many of which you may not want. If you search for pasta OR salad OR dough you will receive all items that contain the word pasta, all items which contain the word salad, and all items which contain the word dough. And, you'll probably get items which contain the word spinach as well!

⊗<Caution>

The more logical search operators you use, the longer it will take Veronica to find the Gopher items you want. Avoid making your logical searches too complex and be sure to use parentheses around any words searched with the OR operator.

Fig. 9.6
No Spinach Please!
Using NOT within your
search will find salad,
sauce, and dough
recipes while eliminat-
ing any that contain
spinach.

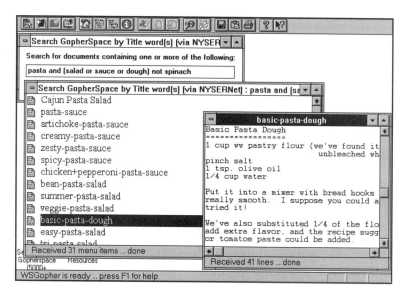

The results are in. Now what?

The items that you receive from a Veronica search are immediately accessible in Gopher. You can save them as bookmarks, view them (if they are
files), or save them as files on your computer. You work with the results of a
Veronica search just like you work with other Gopher menus. For example:

- To save a bookmark to an item, you can select an item by clicking on it
  once and then choosing Add Bookmark from the WSGopher Bookmark
  menu.

- To view a file, just double-click on the menu item.

- To save a file that you are viewing to your computer, just select Save
  Item from the WSGopher File menu.

- Any program archive files that have the .zip extension can be saved to
  your computer by simply double-clicking on the item.

Other places to find Veronica

So far we've tried some searches using Veronica from the University of
Illinois Gopher server. Veronica is a very popular service and there may be

times when the Illinois menu is not available to you or when it is too busy. There are some additional Gopher servers that you can visit to do your Veronica searches. It is also possible to access a Veronica server directly and bypass the "middle man" when submitting your search.

Veronica's Home server

One Gopher that you might want to explore is the Home Veronica server at the University of Nevada (where Veronica was written). To go directly to the Nevada Gopher:

1 Select <u>N</u>ew Gopher item from WSGopher's <u>F</u>ile menu.

2 Type **futique.scs.unr.edu** in the Server Name text box and press Enter.

3 Select the Search All of Gopherspace (5000+ Gophers) Using Veronica menu item. This menu gives you access to a number of search possibilities. Look at figure 9.7 to see what's on the menu.

Fig. 9.7
The Gopher server at the University of Nevada is a good place to gain access to some Veronica servers

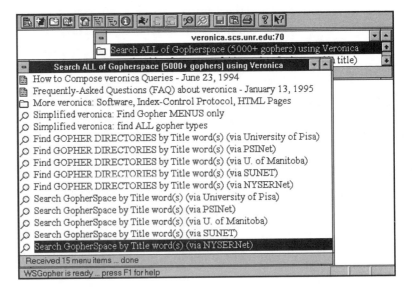

Some of the menu items shown in figure 9.7 that you might find useful include:

- **Simplified Veronica: Find Gopher Menus Only**—This Veronica search only looks for Gopher items that are menus of more items. A simplified search tries all Veronica servers it knows about until it finds one available to process your request. This way you don't have to try each of the individual servers if one or more are busy.

- **Simplified Veronica: Find All Gopher Types**—This Veronica search will find all kinds of Gopher information. It also uses the simplified search method that tries all the Veronica servers it knows about until it finds one that is not busy.

- **Find Gopher Directories by Title Word(s)**—There are several menus of this type which all specify an individual Veronica server name. If you use one of these search items, the specified Veronica server only looks for Gopher items that are menus of more items.

- **Search Gopherspace by Title Word(s)**—There are several menus that let you use an individual Veronica server to search for all kinds of Gopher items.

Veronica via the Mother of all Gophers

Another possibility for accessing Veronica is to go to the Mother of all Gophers, **gopher.tc.umn.edu**. To go directly to the Minnesota Gopher, select New Gopher item from WSGopher's File menu. Type **gopher.tc.umn.edu** in the Server Name text box and press Enter. Once connected, you will see a menu named Other Gopher and Information Services. Double-click on that item to select it and you find one item for searching Gopherspace and a Veronica menu that leads to a display very similar to the University of Nevada menu.

(Tip)

> Be aware that because this is the ancestor of all Gophers and the one that many Gopher clients point to by default, it's a busy site and often quite hard to get to.

Even more Veronica servers

The Veronica servers that are listed in both the Universities of Nevada and Minnesota menus are not the only servers available. The Washington and Lee

University Gopher server supports a menu of Veronica servers including several that are on neither the Nevada or Minnesota sites.

Washington and Lee's Veronica menu is a very nice service that lists the most accessible Veronica servers from the top down. The menu also lists Veronicas that ordinarily may be available, but which have not answered recently. You'll find this list at the server name **liberty.uc.wlu.edu** under the menu Finding Gopher Resources and Search Gopher Menus by Veronica (see fig. 9.8.).

Fig. 9.8
The WLU Veronica menu lists the most responsive servers at the top of the menu.

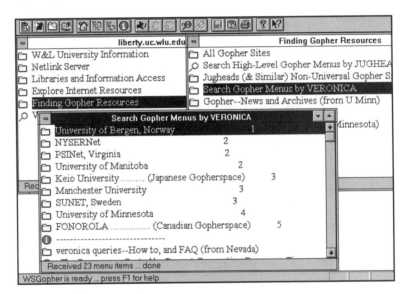

Some servers worth noting on the menu in figure 9.8 are those at Manchester University (United Kingdom), FONOROLA (searches only Canadian Gopherspace), and Keio University (searches only Japanese Gopherspace).

If you are in the U.S., it's best to try the Manchester server in the afternoon or evening, because it will be even later in the day there. Because they don't index worldwide Gopherspace, the FONOROLA and Keio Veronicas should work faster for you if you are looking for Gopher items from either Canada or Japan.

If you select one of the listed servers, you will see another menu with the various search options listed. The nice thing about this next menu is that the server searches are organized by various search types, making it extremely simple to use Veronica (and not requiring you to remember all of the search commands that are talked about earlier in this chapter).

Fig. 9.9
WLU Veronica Search menu provides you with several different searching possibilities.

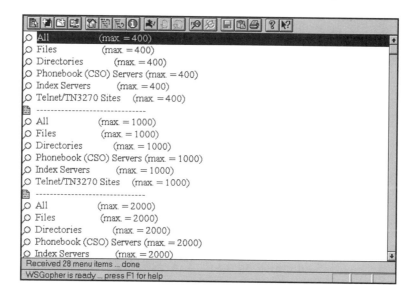

There are five search types you can do on this menu and there are three sets of these search items. The five items, as you can see in figure 9.9, are:

- **All**—Select this menu item to submit a Veronica search that will look for all kinds of items.

- **Files**—Use this menu item to submit a search that will only look for files. This search is like using a -t0 command with a standard Veronica search.

- **Directories**—This menu item submits a search that will only look for menus of additional Gopher items. This search is like using a -t1 command with a Veronica search.

- **Phonebook (CSO) Servers**—Use this item to look for on-line phone books. This search is like using a -t2 command with a Veronica search.

- **Telnet/TN3270 Sites**—Select this menu item to look for Gopher items that use Telnet or TN3270 programs to contact other Internet services. This search is like using a -t8T command with a Veronica search.

The first five of these search items also say (max=400) in the menu item title. These will only look for up to 400 items, like using the command -m400 with a standard Veronica search. The second five look for up to 1000 items (like using -m1000), and the third set look for up to 2000 items (like using -m2000).

Accessing Veronica servers directly

If you know the location of a Veronica server you can access it directly. The advantage of doing so is that you don't have to go through a "middle man" Gopher like those at the University of Illinois, or University of Minnesota. To give you a head start on Veronica searching, the following table lists a number of servers.

Server	Server name and address
Commonly referenced Veronica servers include:	
NYSERNet	**empire.nysernet.org**
PSINet	**info.psi.net**
SUNET (Sweden)	**veronica.sunet.se**
University of Manitoba	**gopher.umanitoba.ca**
UNINETT/University of Bergen	**veronica.uib.no**
University of Pisa	**serra.unipi.it**
University of Cologne	**veronica.uni-koeln.de**
Other Veronica Servers include:	
Manchester University	**info.mcc.ac.uk**
University of Minnesota (alternate Veronica)	**soundgarden.micro.umn.edu**
FONOROLA (Canadian Gopherspace)	**nis.fonorola.net**
Keio University (Japanese Gopherspace)	**veronica.cc.keio.ac.jp**
AARNET (Australian Gopherspace)	**archie.au**

Other Veronica Servers include:	
America Online	**pand03.prod.aol.net**
SURFnet, Netherlands	**info.nic.surfnet.nl**
Tachyon Communications, Florida	**pulsar.tach.net**
University of Stuttgart (German Gopherspace)	**info2.rus.uni-stuttgart.de**
University of Texas, Dallas	**veronica.utdallas.edu**
University of New Brunswick	**sol-alt1.csd.unb.ca**
CNR Milano (Only for Italian Gopherspace)	**gopher.mi.cnr.it**
ASU Veronica Server	**info.asu.edu**
MRNet	**veronica.MR.Net**
Cygnus Telecomm	**veronica.cygnus.nb.ca**

To use one of the Veronica servers listed in the table, you can:

1 Select File, New Gopher item.

2 When the Fetch This Gopher Item dialog box appears, type the server address in the Server Name text box.

3 Type **2347** in the Server Port text box.

4 Type your Veronica search request in the Selector text box (see fig. 9.10).

5 Click the OK button or press Enter.

This action actually submits the search request you typed in the Selector text box directly to a Veronica server that is running on the computer specified in the Server Name text box.

If you get a message that says Connection Refused, it probably means that the server is busy. However, it might mean that the server does not accept public requests and you must be part of that network to use that server. (America Online's Veronica is an example—to use it you must be a member logged on to its service.)

66 *Plain English, please!*

The **port number** used in the previous example is a way for an Internet computer to tell what kind of program is trying to connect to it. Usually, a Gopher client connects to an Internet computer using port number 70, which indicates a Gopher server. The port number 2347 is the standard way of communicating with a Veronica server. 99

Fig. 9.10
Using a Veronica server directly can provide you faster or easier access for searching.

Tip

One way to find active Veronica servers is to use Veronica to search for them. You can look for the word veronica and only search for Gopher index items. An easy way to accomplish this task is to use one of the Veronica searches on Washington and Lee University's menu (**liberty.uc.wlu.edu**) and select a text index search. When you use a Veronica search that looks for all kinds of items, you can type **-t7 veronica** to find only the text index items.

How can I keep up with the latest Veronica developments?

Veronica is a relatively new addition to Gopherspace and improvements are ongoing in the Veronica software and in providing access to Veronica. There are several options available for you to keep up with the latest developments.

The Veronica FAQ file

A Veronica Frequently Asked Questions (FAQ) file is maintained by Steven Foster at the University of Nevada. You can view a copy at the following location: **futique.scs.unr.edu** under the Search All Gopherspace (5000+) Using Veronica menu, in the Frequently Asked Questions about Veronica (FAQ) file. This file is updated as new developments in the Veronica service occur.

The Home Veronica server

The Veronica FAQ is maintained on the Home Veronica server (**futique.scs.unr.edu**). The server itself has other items about Veronica, including the server software distribution point and a pointer to a Veronica World Wide Web page. Browse the More Veronica item on the Veronica search menu if you want to learn more about the technical side of Veronica.

The comp.infosystems.gopher newsgroup

To keep abreast of all the latest developments in Gopherspace, don't overlook the UseNet news group, **comp.infosystems.gopher**. If you have access to UseNet, finding this group should be easy. There is a wide range of areas of discussion. People post questions and answers about using Gopher, information on new developments in Gopher software, and new services that become available via Gopher. Those with a technical inclination have the opportunity to learn about many of the ins and outs of Gopher and its components.

10

Searching with Archie

Wouldn't you like to find some free stuff out there on the Internet? You can find these programs and documents by using Archie—a powerful tool available on Gopher.

Internet computers hold massive amounts of documents, images, and programs just waiting to be discovered. Finding these files and programs, however, is a real challenge if you don't know where to look. Fortunately, Archie can help you locate them.

Introducing Archie

Archie was one of the first programs to make Internet-based information and programs organized and accessible. It started as a way for McGill University to distribute software and files online to its faculty and students. The usefulness of Archie soon became obvious and its use expanded to the role it plays today as a searchable database of anonymous FTP archives.

Plain English, please!

The term **anonymous FTP** refers to the process of retrieving files from Internet sites. FTP stands for file transfer protocol. When managers of Internet computers want to make files publicly available, they allow "anonymous" users to log on to their computers in order to download those files. The kinds of programs available range from very clever games to Internet programs like WSGopher.

The standing of Archie in the Internet community is reflected by the naming of the two programs we learned about in the previous two chapters. While the Archie software got its name as a variant of "archive," Veronica and Jughead followed Archie and formed a set of names similar to those of some famous comic book characters. This may just be an indication of the literary tastes of computer programmers, but you can also see the names as representing a family of similar Internet search programs.

How Archie works

At the heart of Archie is the server software. Archie servers regularly read the directories of anonymous FTP sites to build a database of available files. The Archie servers are also able to search those databases after they're built.

Most Archie servers let you log in directly and submit searches. There is another way to access Archie as well. Just as Gopher clients can talk to Gopher servers, there are Archie clients that can talk to Archie servers. The way you use Archie from Gopher can involve either of these two access methods (see fig. 10.1). There is a Gopher to Archie gateway that can submit searches directly from Gopher in the same way that an Archie client would. Gopher can also be used as a jumping off point to connect to Archie servers via Telnet. We'll talk about both methods in this chapter.

Fig. 10.1
Archie servers can be used with an Archie client or accessed directly via Telnet. Gopher can help you use Archie both ways.

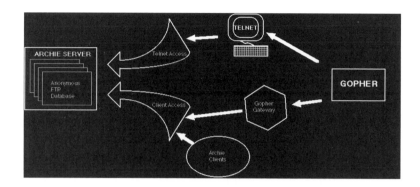

When you submit an Archie search, the characters that you specify are matched against entries in Archie's index. Archie sends back a list of any file or directory names that match. Archie also lets you use some commands to control the scope of your search and the number of files to look for. The items it finds appear as normal Gopher items. After you find something you're interested in, you have a few options. You can:

- View it (if it's a text file)

- Download it (if it's a program file)

- Select it for further exploration (if it's a directory on an FTP site)

The way that Archie works sounds a lot like Veronica and Jughead. This is because Veronica was patterned after some of the concepts that are found in Archie, and Jughead was patterned after Veronica. The difference between them is that Archie is used to index anonymous FTP archives throughout the world, while Veronica let's you search for items on Gophers throughout the world, and Jughead only searches one particular Gopher server.

Three ways to search with Archie

There are three ways you can conduct an Archie search:

- **An exact search**. You can submit a word or character string, and Archie will try to find names which match the exact order and case of those characters. If, for example, you want to find directories containing Windows software, you might submit an exact search for the word **Windows**.

- **A substring search**. You can try to find a word or character string that is part of a larger word or name. Archie will try to find names which match the characters whether they are upper- or lowercase. It also matches names that contain characters before or after the set that you submit. A substring search on **windows** might find MSwindows, or windows3, or even MSwindows3.

- **A regular expression search**. You can submit a substring of characters that include some unknown characters (called wild cards) that can match a number of possibilities. The name "regular expression" is a phrase borrowed from UNIX and represents a way of matching complex strings of characters. This type of search is useful when you want to find files based on two or more substrings. For example, you might want to find files with win in the file name, followed by some other characters, followed by the substring zip. This type of search might find winsock.zip or winning zip or even twin zippers (OK, I made these last two up, but you get the idea).

66 *Plain English, please!*

When computer programmers talk about sets of letters, numbers, and punctuation, they use the term **string**. A string, in computer terms, is any set of single characters that are strung together. A word by itself is a string and a word in combination with numbers or other characters, like punctuation, is also a string. 2-trains-on-track-9! is a string containing words, numbers, and punctuation.

A **substring** is part of a larger string. Win is a substring of Windows. indo is also a substring of Windows because it matches exactly the order and case of some of the characters in the word, Windows. 99

Using an exact Archie search

You can try out some Archie searches by using WSGopher's Home server at the University of Illinois. The University of Illinois Gopher menu should appear automatically when you start WSGopher. If it does not:

1 Select File, New Gopher Item.

2 When you see the Fetch this Gopher Item dialog box, type **gopher.uiuc.edu** in the Server Name text box and press Enter (see fig. 10.2).

Fig. 10.2
You can use the New Gopher Item function of WSGopher to connect to the University of Illinois Gopher server via the Fetch this Gopher Item dialog box.

After you are there, you can begin your search:

1 From the Illinois Gopher menu, select the Internet File Server (FTP) Sites menu item.

2 Next, you will see an item named Search of Most FTP Sites (Archie). When you select this item you should see a WSGopher search box. You can now try an exact Archie search.

3 In the box, type **-e tetris**. The -e tells Archie to do an exact search and tetris is what we'll look for. In case you don't know, Tetris is a popular computer game that was invented in Russia.

 (Tip)

> Why does the menu say Internet File Server Sites? In Internet terms, a file server is a computer system whose job is to distribute computer files. Usually, people retrieve files from these servers via anonymous FTP, however, you can retrieve files through Gopher as well.

When you press Enter, the Gopher server submits your Archie search. It may take a few minutes, but when the search is done, you'll see a list of items like the one shown in figure 10.3.

Fig. 10.3
These are some items
returned by an exact
Archie search for tetris.

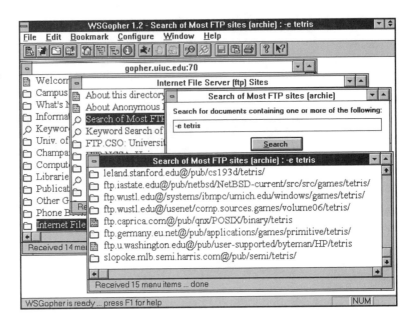

You can see in this example that an exact search for tetris finds mostly
directories and that there are not a whole lot of these items—only 15 were
found. One of these directories might contain the game that you are looking
for, but considering the popularity of Tetris, you would expect to find a lot
more versions. You need a way to expand the scope of the search.

Using an Archie substring search

A substring search of Archie expands the scope of a search by matching
more items. Instead of finding files or directories that exactly match the word
tetris, a substring search returns any items that contain tetris anywhere
within their name. To try this out, you can again use the Archie search from
the University of Illinois. This time, type **-s tetris** in the search box. The -s
tells Archie to perform a substring search (see fig. 10.4).

Fig. 10.4

More items are returned by an Archie substring search for tetris than by an exact search.

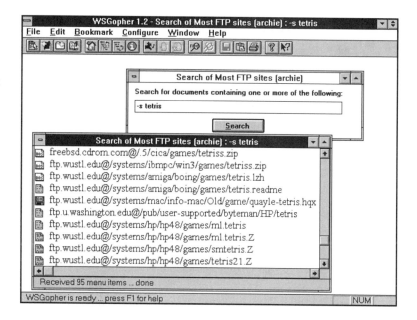

This time we find 95 items and the type of items is much more varied. There are some files and some directories. By scrolling down this list, you see different versions of the Tetris game for DOS, Amiga, Macintosh, and Hewlett-Packard UNIX systems. You can interpret this listing by looking at the various parts of each line:

- An icon tells you the type of file. In figure 10.4, the icons represent three DOS archive files, a text file, a Macintosh archive, two more text files, and three UNIX files.

- Following the icon is the address of the FTP server followed by an At sign (@).

- After the At sign is the path to the directory where the file is stored.

- The last part of the line is the name of the file.

We can see the effect of the substring search by looking at the file names found: tetriss.zip, tetris.lzh, quayle-tetris.hqx, ml.tetris.Z, and tetris21.Z. These all contain tetris and represent a lot more variety than we found with an exact Archie search. You can click on any of these items for download, but, of course, only the DOS archives are useful to a WSGopher user.

❶ *(Tip)*

Computer files have names that sometimes are only slightly related to their content. For example, the latest version of WSGopher is distributed as wsg-12.exe. You would have to know that name in advance to do an exact or even a substring search for it. Many times, however, you'll find out about a file or program from someone else who gives you the archived name as well. This makes it easier to find the file through Archie. Archie also matches directory names; so if you are looking for a common piece of software, like Kermit, you might find a bunch of Kermit directories out on FTP sites.

By default, the University of Illinois Archie search submits the substring version, so we did not have to use the -s command. But searches done from other Gopher servers might require the -s for a substring search. Another default of this Gopher search is to return only the first 95 items it finds. We can increase this number by adding the -m command to our search. If you want your search to return 200 items, you would type -s tetris -m 200 in the search box.

Doing a regular expression search

Sometimes a substring search doesn't let you be specific enough. This is where a regular expression search comes in handy. For example, you might be looking for a particular version number of Tetris. You might use the following search to find such a file: -r tetris[0-9].*. Let's look at the different parts of a regular expression search:

- -r means do a regular expression search.

- tetris is a substring that should be part of the item name.

- [0-9] means match any single occurrence of the characters within the brackets. In this case, we'll look for a number which ranges from 0 to 9.

- . means match any single character.

- * means match any number of the previous character (so .* means match any number of any character)

When you look at the output from this search, you see different files than in the previous examples (see fig. 10.5).

Fig. 10.5
A regular expression search allows you to be more specific and find different kinds of files.

```
Search of Most FTP sites [archie] : -r tetris[0-9].*
gatekeeper.dec.com@/.b/usenet/comp.sources.games/volume6/sun-tetris2/
freebsd.cdrom.com@/.5/cica/games/tetris11.zip
ftp.wustl.edu@/systems/atari/umich.edu/8bit/Games/tetris3d.com
ftp.wustl.edu@/systems/atari/umich.edu/8bit/New/.in.tetris3d.com
ftp.wustl.edu@/usenet/comp.sources.games/volume15/gtetris2/
ftp.wustl.edu@/usenet/comp.sources.games/volume15/gtetris3/
ftp.wustl.edu@/usenet/comp.sources.games/volume18/gtetris4/
ftp.wustl.edu@/usenet/comp.sources.games/volume06/sun-tetris2/
usc.edu@/archive/usenet/sources/comp.sources.games/volume18/gtetris4/
usc.edu@/archive/usenet/sources/comp.sources.games/volume15/gtetris2/
usc.edu@/archive/usenet/sources/comp.sources.games/volume15/gtetris3/
usc.edu@/archive/usenet/sources/comp.sources.games/volume17/gtetris3/
Received 30 menu items ... done
```

One of the interesting things that this search turned up was tetris3d, a three-dimensional version of Tetris. You can see how, by being more specific in your search, you have an even better chance of finding what you need.

(Tip)

> Because regular expression searches take the most work by the Archie server, they may take a little longer than an exact or substring search. If you get a message saying the server is too busy, or if the search doesn't return any items when you would expect at least a few, just try your search again.

Other places to use Archie on Gopher

If you can't access the University of Illinois Gopher or you don't find an Archie search on the Home Gopher you usually use, there are a couple of remote Gophers you might try.

One menu you might want to visit to use an Archie search is the University of Minnesota Gopher, **gopher.tc.umn.edu**. Select the New Gopher Item under WSGopher's File menu like we did in figure 10.2, but this time type **gopher.tc.umn.edu** in the Server Name text box. On the Minnesota Gopher menu you will see an item named Internet File Server (FTP) Sites. Double-click this menu to select it and you will see that there are two items on the menu for an Archie search. One is labeled gopher+ version and the other is non-gopher+ version.

Gopher+ is an extension to the way basic Gopher clients and servers operate and provides a few more Gopher features, like the ability of the Gopher server to ask for information from you via a window on your Gopher client. Although WSGopher does support Gopher plus features, the gopher+ version of the Archie search on the University of Minnesota Gopher is unreliable and may not work for you. For the most consistent result, use the non-gopher+ search item.

> This is a busy site because a lot of Gopher servers point to the University of Minnesota Gopher to provide their Archie searches. It's a good place to explore if other sites are unavailable, but it may take patience to accomplish a search.

You can also look for similar menus on other popular Gopher servers. One example is the University of Utah Gopher, **gopher.scs.unr.edu**. From the opening menu, look in Other Gophers and Internet Services and select the Search FTP Site Lists via Archie menu. This menu has items that allow you to conduct Archie exact searches as well as Archie substring searches without your needing to use the -e or -s commands.

> One way to find Archie on Gopher is to use Veronica. You can search on the word Archie and look for menu items, Gopher searches, or Telnet items. To find menu items, use the search **–t1 archie**. To find search items with the name Archie in their title, use **–t7 archie**. For Telnet items, use the search **–t8 archie**.

Telnet to Archie servers via Gopher

Let's use WSGopher's New Gopher Item (Ctrl+N) feature to visit the University of New Mexico Gopher, whose server name is **lib.nmsu.edu.** From the opening menu, select the Archie, Jughead, Veronica, WAIS, Netfind/Archie (search anonymous FTP sites) menu. You will see several Telnet items that each point to a different Archie server. When you select one of these items, your Gopher client program starts up an external Telnet program which will make the connection to the remote Archie computer on the Internet.

Plain English, please!

Netfind is an Internet program that helps you find e-mail addresses by searching with a person's name, geographical location, and institution name.

If the connection is made successfully, you should see a `login:` prompt in the Telnet screen. You should type **archie** and press Enter. If you see a `password:` prompt, just press Enter again. If the logon to the Archie server is successful, you will eventually see an `archie>` prompt and you can then enter commands. Sometimes the Archie server is too busy to accept your session, and it gives you a message to that effect. You must try again or try a different server. When you do see the `archie>` prompt, you can type the **find** command followed by the name of a program or file you are interested in. This process is shown in figure 10.6.

Fig. 10.6
A Telnet session to Archie can help you find programs and files.

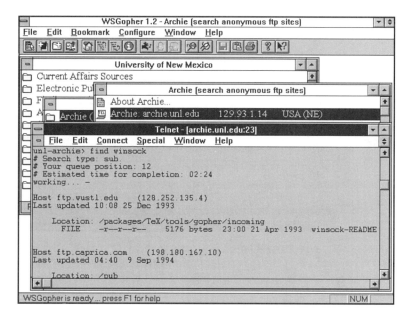

⊗<Caution> | In order to use Telnet via Gopher, you must be sure that Gopher can find your Telnet application. Select <u>C</u>onfigure from the WSGopher menu, and then select <u>T</u>elnet/3270 Path and hit the browse button at the left of the Telnet program text box to point WSGopher to your Telnet application.

Using the Archie server

After you get the `archie>` prompt you can start using the Archie server to find files. The simplest way to do this is to type the **find** followed by the name or partial name of a file you want to find. After you press Enter, Archie lets you know that it is processing your search. If it finds anything, it lists the locations and names of the files on the screen. By default, the Archie server performs a substring search. If you wish to change your search method from the `archie>` prompt, you may do so:

- Type **set search exact** before using the **find** command to conduct an exact search.

- Type **set search regex** before using the **find** command to conduct a regular expression search.

- If you are conducting an exact or regex search, type **set search sub** before using the **find** command to return to a substring search.

Some other sites with Archie Telnet access

If, for some reason, you can't access the University of New Mexico Gopher, try another Gopher server that offers Archie Telnet access. The following table lists some of these servers:

Gopher	Menu path
inform.umd.edu	From the first menu, select Access to Other Electronic Information Resources, and then select Archie File Searching Service.
gopher.tamu.edu	On the opening menu, under WORLD-WIDE INFORMA-TION, select Browse by Subject, then select Internet (UseNet, WAIS, WWW, and so on), and finally select Archie (Searching Anonymous FTP Sites).
gopher.uchicago.edu	From the first menu, select ...SEARCH the Internet (by Veronica, Jughead, Archie, WAIS, WWW, ...), and then select SEARCH FTP sites—Internet file and archive servers.

Interpreting the Archie output

If Archie finds some matches to your search request, it lists some information about the name and location of the file in the Telnet window. An example output might read as follows:

```
Host gatekeeper.dec.com  (15.1.0.2)

Last updated 16:37  8 Sep 1994

Location:  /.3/net/infosys/gopher/Windows
      FILE  -rw--r--r--  320705 bytes 19:53  9 May 1994
wsg-10.exe
```

There are several elements of this output you should make note of and copy:

- **Host address** (the name of the anonymous FTP site). The Host address in our example is **gatekeeper.dec.com**

- **Location** (the directory on the FTP site where the file is located). In this example, the Location is **/net/infosys/gopher/windows**

- **File name**. In this case, the file name is **wsg-10.exe**

You may have noticed that, although the example shows the directory path as /.3/net/infosys/gopher/Windows, we told you that the file could actually be found in /net/infosys/gopher/Windows. This is because, generally, directories which begin with a . are invisible and cannot be accessed by anonymous FTP. When you see a path like this, the first directory not preceded by a . will be the first one you see.

The filename is usually at the end of some information that includes the date the file was created. You can use the site, location, and name to retrieve a file via an anonymous FTP session, if that service is available to you, or you can retrieve the file via Gopher.

Using Gopher to retrieve files from anonymous FTP sites

We've already seen a couple of items that would allow us to try to retrieve an anonymous FTP file via Gopher. On the University of Minnesota Gopher menu, there is a Query a Specific FTP Host item. This is a **Gopher to FTP gateway**. If you select it, it gives you a box to type in the FTP site's name (the host name as we discussed above). If it can make the connection, you will then see a menu item that represents that FTP site. You can select it and follow the directory path you discovered from the Archie search until you find the file you need.

 Plain English, please!

> In computer terms, a gateway is a piece of software that passes information between two kinds of networks or two kinds of software. A **Gopher to FTP gateway** will let anonymous FTP files and directories be displayed from within Gopher. The gateway acts as an intermediary (what we used to call a middle man) that translates a Gopher request into an FTP command and then translates the FTP file listing back into a Gopher menu.

Other useful sources for FTP sites are menus like the Internet File Server (FTP) Sites on the University of Illinois Gopher server. You may be able to find your FTP host within this kind of menu that allows access to FTP sites directly from Gopher. The example we used in the previous section, wsg-12.exe, can be found this way as you can see in figure 10.7. First look for the FTP server name, **gatekeeper.dec.com**, and then follow the directory path, which leads you to the net/infosys/gopher/Windows directory. As you can see, you don't necessarily have to leave Gopher to retrieve a file from an FTP site.

Fig. 10.7
Using a Gopher to FTP
gateway to retrieve
files.

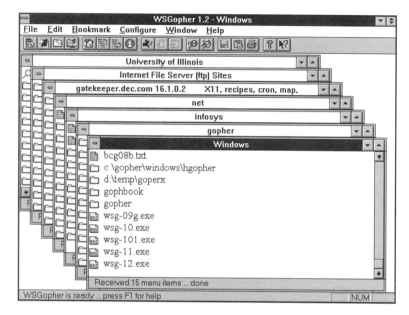

A final word

Archie is a very popular Internet service. With persistence, it's possible to do a direct Gopher to Archie search, but sometimes it's much easier to go the Telnet item route. But even with one "external" Telnet excursion, we've seen that we can accomplish a lot by just using the capabilities found within Gopher. Hopefully, the Gopher to Archie gateway will continue to see improvement so that these types of Gopher searches will be easier to access and easier to do.

11

Searching with WAIS

*The mass of informa-
tion available in
WAIS databases is at
your fingertips when
you use Gopher.*

In this chapter:

• An introduction to document searching with WAIS

• The kinds of documents available

• Search WAIS databases using Gopher

I f you've ever used an Internet accessible library card catalog such as MAGIC (the computer catalog at Michigan State University which you can use to find books, authors, or topics available through their library holdings), you may have been amazed that you could search for a book and see that it was available in a library halfway around the world. Wouldn't it be great if you could then get the text of that book on your computer screen or search for chapters that have the information that you want? WAIS (pronounced "ways") was developed with just such a vision in mind.

A brief introduction to WAIS

WAIS, which stands for Wide Area Information Servers, was originally developed at a company called Thinking Machines Corporation, which made large parallel processing computer systems. (A parallel processing computer is one that has a large number of processors working together on one task.) It's not surprising that Thinking Machines' computers were well-suited to the tasks necessary to maintain and search WAIS databases.

WAIS is based on a protocol that allows searching collections of text. This protocol was developed as a standard to allow different kinds of computers to easily exchange text information over the Internet. It defines a method of searching large text databases for certain keywords and transmitting the results over the network.

 Plain English, please!

A **protocol** is a set of rules that computers or other devices use to transmit information back and forth. Just like governments have diplomatic protocols that define how they are supposed to act when dealing with international issues, computer programs use protocols that define how they will act when they transmit information over the Internet. **"**

There are over 700 WAIS document databases available through Gopher. They range from literary collections to indexed collections of messages from popular UseNet newsgroups. Each database is typically maintained by a different individual or organization, but they are drawn together into online collections that make easy access to a diverse set of information.

How is WAIS different from Veronica, Archie, and Jughead?

Jughead, Veronica, and Archie are programs that search for documents, files, and services that are available somewhere on the Internet. WAIS databases are indexed collections of documents available on the Internet which can be individually searched. In other words, you use Jughead, Veronica, and Archie, to search for and find some information. With WAIS, first you find a database on a particular topic, and then you use WAIS to search it.

How WAIS works

A WAIS database consists of an indexed collection of documents. When you search a WAIS database, your search words are compared with the words in that particular index. The index points to any documents that contain the words matching your search and the WAIS software transmits a list of document titles to you electronically. You can then browse the individual documents.

 Plain English, please!

> A **database** is a large collection of computerized information (usually called data) that is organized for quick retrieval. This is done by creating an index to the data which uses just a word or abbreviation (called a keyword) to represent an item. Searching the index is a quick process because there is no need to look at every word in the database—just keywords. When your search word matches a keyword, the database software can quickly find the data pointed to by that index entry. Your bank has a database that tracks your balance. Your bank account number is actually the keyword that identifies your particular balance and account information.

WAIS can use the same client-server approach that many Internet programs use to communicate. There are WAIS clients available that let you create and transmit a search request to a WAIS server. The client is then able to display any information it receives in a format you can read on the screen. Gopher can also act as a WAIS client (which is why this chapter is in this book!).

When you use WAIS databases via Gopher, you submit your search like any other Gopher text search. You select the search item, and Gopher prompts you to type in one or more search words. When you do a Gopher WAIS search, WAIS finds documents that contain each word individually. In other words, if you type in **cat dog** when asked what to search for, WAIS finds documents that contain either cat or dog.

You might be asking yourself, "If you search for cat AND dog, aren't these two different searches?" Remember that a WAIS database is a collection of documents, so if you conduct a search on a WAIS database by typing in **cat dog**, the search will return any documents that contain either the words cat or dog. You can think of the documents as being like individual chapters within a book and the search process like looking in the index for the occurrence of particular words in the text.

Viewing WAIS on the University of Minnesota Gopher

On many Gophers you will find a menu item named Other Gopher and Information Servers. If you choose that item, you will usually see another item entitled WAIS Based Information. These usually point to the University of Minnesota Gopher menus of the same name at **gopher.tc.umn.edu**. (In Gopherspace, all roads seem to lead to Minnesota!)

To find this menu in WSGopher, select File, New Gopher Item. Then type **gopher.tc.umn.edu** in the Server name text box and press Enter or click OK. Double-click on Other Gopher and Information Servers, and then double-click on WAIS Based Information. The first item on this menu is List of All WAIS Sources, which gives you immediate access to all 700 or so WAIS databases (see fig. 11.1).

Fig. 11.1
The WAIS Gopher menu at the University of Minnesota has a wide variety of text databases that you can search.

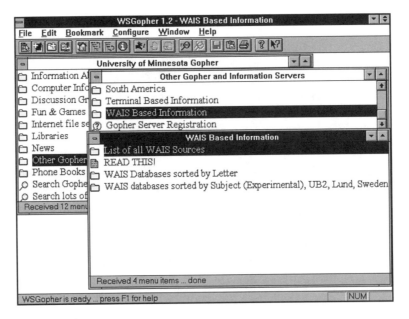

If you decide to look at all the databases by double-clicking on List of all WAIS Sources, you'll see that they are listed in alphabetical order, much like a phone book (see fig. 11.2). To conduct a search:

1 Scroll through this list by using the down arrow or the scroll bar at the right of the window until you come to the Ws. These are all search items.

2 Select one, such as the White-House-Papers.src, by double-clicking on that item.

3 You will be prompted to enter a search term. (If you get a box titled Select Extended View, just double-click on Directory, and you will then see the search box.)

4 Type in **health** and press Enter or click on the Search button and the search will start.

5 When the search is done, you'll see a list of document files related to health issues. You can now begin browsing any of the retrieved items.

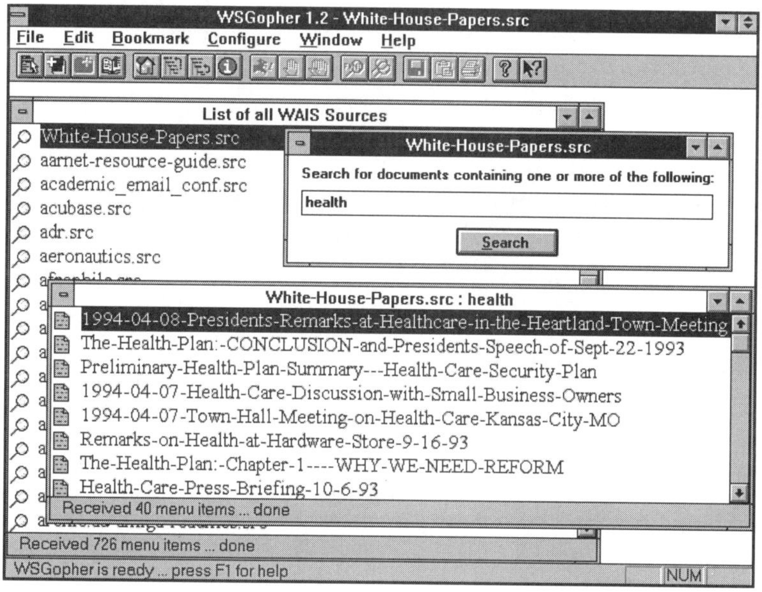

Fig. 11.2

It's easy to access a WAIS search. Searching the White-House-Papers for the word health will show you many document titles, each of which can be read individually.

WAIS sorted by letter

As you can imagine, it often takes quite a while to load 700 menu items in Gopher. If you don't want to look at the whole list, you may want to choose the WAIS Databases sorted by Letter instead of the List of All WAIS Sources. To do so:

A random sampling of WAIS information

If you browse the list of databases, you'll soon find that it's quite diverse. A bunch of items early in the list start with the letters ANU. ANU stands for Australian National University and these databases contain information on topics dealing with Asia and the Pacific region. Other random sightings include the Book of Mormon, the NOAA Environmental Services Data Directory, a Science Fiction Series–Guide, U.S. State Department Travel Advisories, cold fusion, higher education software, and a UNIX manual.

Some other databases you might find interesting are listed in the following table:

Database	Description
USHOUSE_house_bill_text_104th.src	The individual bills introduced during the 104th session of the U.S. House of Representatives
higher-education-software.src	A collection of abstracts listing educational software from many fields
ibm.pc.FAQ.src	Frequently asked questions about IBM PC systems
jargon.src	An online dictionary of computer jargon
k-12-software.src	A collection of abstracts listing educational software for students in kindergarten through high school
macintosh-tidbits.src	An online newsletter of Macintosh-related information
movie-reviews.src	An online collection of movie reviews
recipes.src	A collection of recipes
smithsonian-pictures.src	A catalog of pictures found in the Smithsonian Institute

1 Close the List of all WAIS Sources window.

2 Double-click on WAIS Databases sorted by Letter. This menu (see fig. 11.3) lets you browse the databases according to the first letter of their title (upper- or lowercase).

3 You can then double-click on the letter containing the database you'd like to search.

Fig. 11.3
WAIS databases organized by letter make it easier and quicker to find a database that you are interested in.

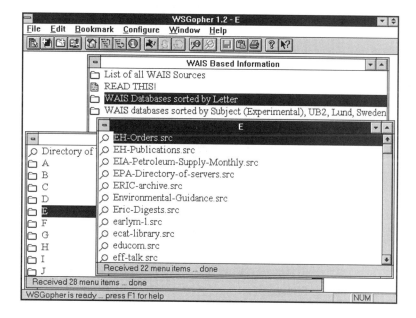

WAIS sorted by subject

Another organized presentation of these databases comes to us from the University of Lund in Sweden. Close the WAIS Databases sorted by Letter window to get back to the WAIS Based Information menu. The last item on this menu, WAIS databases sorted by Subject (Experimental) leads to a compilation of the WAIS databases by subject (see fig. 11.4).

Fig. 11.4
The University of Lund in Sweden provides a menu of WAIS databases organized by subject.

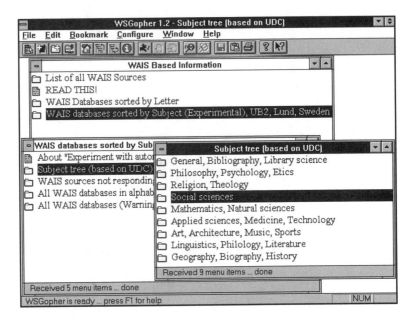

As you can tell from the menu title, this is currently an experimental service—it is still being developed. This means that the look and operation of the menus might change in the future. The current menu represents a project that automatically detects and classifies new WAIS databases as they become available on the Internet. They also list databases that may not be presently responding to searches.

1 Double-click on the WAIS databases sorted by Subject (Experimental) item.

2 You'll find the classified list of databases under Subject tree (based on UDC) menu. Double-click on this item.

3 The organization of subjects is based on the Universal Decimal Classification (UDC), which is a British library cataloging system similar to the U.S. Dewey Decimal system. Double-click on any item to begin exploring.

The subject menu of WAIS sources is run from the University of Lund in Sweden. They use an automated process to discover and classify new WAIS databases. This explains why they use the European UDC system for classifying information instead of the Dewey Decimal system or the Library of Congress system.

Examples of a WAIS search

You can get a better understanding of WAIS searches by looking at several example databases. As already mentioned, doing a search using WAIS is like any other Gopher search you've done in the past.

1 Select an item and type in your search words, following the tips and examples you've already seen.

2 Click the Search button.

Let's go through the search process for several different WAIS databases so that you can get a feel for how you might find information from different sources.

Name that tune

One of the databases available through WAIS is a catalog of sheet music. You might be wondering what the exact title of one of Richard Rodgers (of Rodgers and Hammerstein fame) songs is. You can search on Rodgers to find what is listed within this database (see fig. 11.5). To try this search:

1 In WSGopher, choose <u>W</u>indow, WAIS Based Information.

2 Double-click on List of all WAIS Sources to see the WAIS databases.

3 In WSGopher, choose <u>E</u>dit, <u>F</u>ind. Type in **sheet_music_index** and click on Find Next. When accessing a lot of information, this is a good shortcut to use.

4 Double-click on Sheet_Music_Index.src. (Double-click on Directory if you see the Select Extended View box.)

5 Type in **rodgers**.

6 Click the Search button.

Fig. 11.5

A search of the Sheet Music catalog database can help you find song titles by different composers.

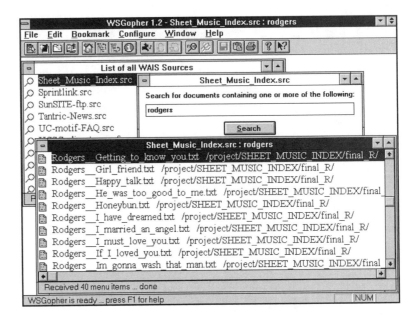

You might notice that Rodgers wrote a couple of songs about love and wonder what other composers wrote about love. To find out:

1 Close the output and search windows.

2 In the search box, double-click on rodgers to highlight the word, and type the word **love**.

3 Click the Search button to see the new results (see fig. 11.6).

Fig. 11.6

Songs about love can be found by using love as your search word.

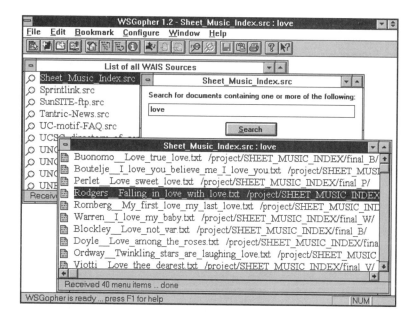

Poetry: poets and poems

MIT has made a collection of poetry available in a WAIS database. As an example of how you might use this database, let's say you want to find poems that use the word rose. You might find out that, in poetry, not only did the rose bloom, but the sun rose as well. Whether you are looking for the flower or the verb, you can find examples in this database.

1 From WSGopher's WAIS Based Information window, double-click on the List of all WAIS Sources menu.

2 Use the Edit and Find procedure described in the earlier section, "Name that tune," and search for the word poetry.

3 Double-click on poetry.src (and double-click on Directory if you see the Select Extended View menu).

4 Type the word **rose** in the search box and click the Search button.

5 You'll then see lists of poems that contain the word rose similar to that displayed in figure 11.7. Double-click on an item to see the actual poem text.

Fig. 11.7
A walk through the poetry database will let you find poems on a particular subject or by a particular poet

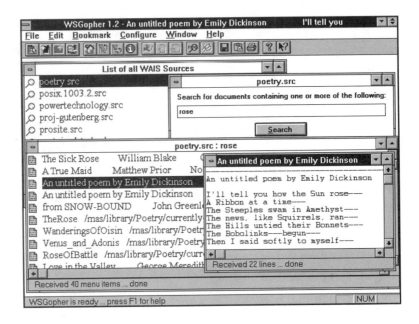

What's the population of Zaire?

If you are wondering about some geographical or political information, you might want to search the World Fact Book WAIS database.

1 From WSGopher's WAIS Based Information window, double-click on the List of all WAIS Sources menu.

2 Use the Edit and Find procedure described earlier in the section, "Name that tune," and search for the word factbook.

3 Double-click on world-factbook.src (and double-click on Directory if you see the Select Extended View menu).

4 Type the word **zaire** in the search box and click the search button.

5 You will receive a number of different document titles in response. If you look at Zaire Geography it tells you the population of that country. (In WSGopher, you can choose Edit, Find to go directly to the population figure.)

Fig. 11.8
Searching the World
Fact Book can provide
you with all kinds of
information about
different countries.

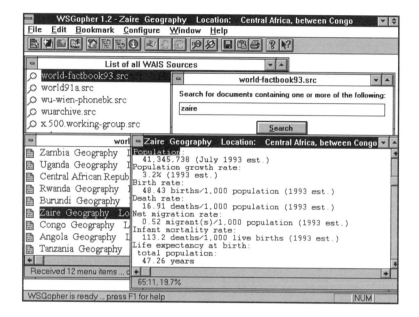

These are just a few examples of what you can find with WAIS. With over 500 databases and an increasing number appearing all the time, the world of online information is getting more extensive. Fortunately for you, it is getting much easier to access at the same time.

Part IV:

Burrowing into Everything

Gophering from Online Services

By now you might be asking, "What about the online services I belong to—can I use Gopher with them?" Yes, you can.

With AOL, you can Gopher to the House of Representatives. CompuServe now provides full Internet access. Today, the major online services let you access Gopher, though it might look slightly different through their interface. But remember, wherever you go, Gopher is Gopher. This chapter takes a look at some of the major online services and how they let you use Gopher.

Online services vs. Internet Service Providers

An **online service** is different than an Internet Service Provider—though the line is becoming blurred lately. Online services give you access to a particular private network of information, files, and services, besides being a gateway to the Internet. You might think of them as cities along the information highway.

Most of these services were offering access to their private networks before they could hook into the Internet. Now you can get to the Net from these online services. Most services provide Internet access from within their traditional software, but that too is changing. CompuServe, for example, now offers Internet service through a separate dial-up number, making it essentially an Internet Service Provider.

Keep in mind that Gopher is a unique part of the Internet, and no matter what face an online service puts on it, Gopher is the same: information organized in lists of directories and files.

Each online service has its strengths and weaknesses, and each appeal to some people for a variety of reasons: look, pricing, speed, content, and so on. You should be able to get free access time to any service before you pay to subscribe. With the free time, you can check out the service before you fork over any real money. Most new computers and modems come with free connection offers. Check magazine ads as well.

America Online

To get to Gopher through America Online, you should have version 2.0 or higher. The examples here use that version of AOL software. You can contact AOL at 800-827-6364.

After you've installed the AOL software and set up your account, choose Internet Connection from the Main Menu window. Figure 12.1 shows you what that window looks like after you're connected to AOL.

From the AOL Internet Connection window, shown in figure 12.2, choose the Gopher & WAIS Databases button. (See Chapter 11, "Searching with WAIS," for more information on that search tool.) AOL then opens its main Gopher window, shown in figure 12.3.

Fig. 12.1
The Internet is one of many options in AOL's service.

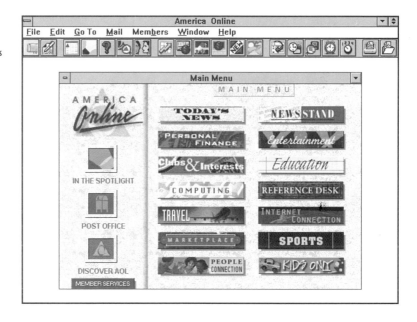

Fig. 12.2
Gopher and WAIS searching are here at the click of a button.

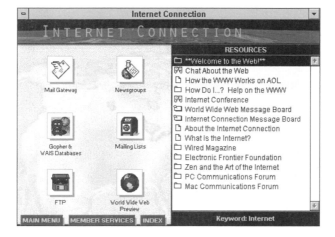

Fig. 12.3
Suddenly, AOL is
beginning to look a
lot like Gopher.

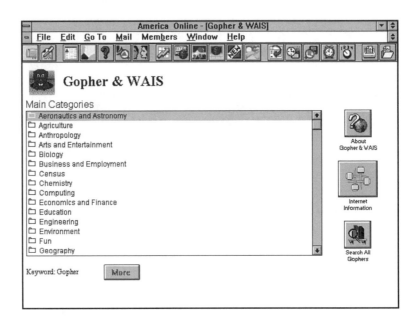

(Tip)

> To get to the AOL Gopher window quickly, you can edit your Favorite Places
> to include an entry linked to the keyword, Gopher. From AOL's main menu,
> choose Go To, Edit Favorite Places, and add a menu entry with the keyword:
> Gopher. Adding this entry lets you get gophering by selecting an item from the
> Go To menu.

From here, the AOL Gopher is point and click. The editors at AOL have set up
Gopher categories at the first-level window. Figure 12.3 shows the main
Gopher window and part of the categories listed there. These categories link
out to Gopherspace.

(Tip)

> Remember, the categories you see here, and the Gopher items in those
> categories, are set up by the editors at AOL. Don't expect to see every Internet
> Gopher listed. If you know how to navigate Gopherspace, though, you can
> find whatever you want.

To start, double-click an item from the list. The next level of information displays just like any Gopher software. For each of the main categories set up by AOL, there is a More button that leads you to other Gopher sites under this category. Figure 12.4 shows the Gopher sites under the category Fun.

Fig. 12.4
Click the More Fun Resources button for lists of other Gopher sites under this category.

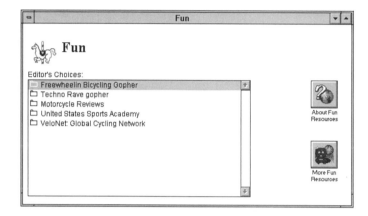

In the Main Gopher window (refer to fig. 12.3), you may have noticed a Search All Gophers button. Clicking here leads you to a Veronica search session that helps you find files throughout Gopherspace. (See Chapter 9, "Searching with Veronica," for more information specifically about Veronica searching.)

Figure 12.5 shows you AOL's Gopher ready to search for items with the term video in their description. To use this tool yourself, enter a search term, and click OK. The Veronica server shows you the results of your search, and you can click on the items you want to investigate further.

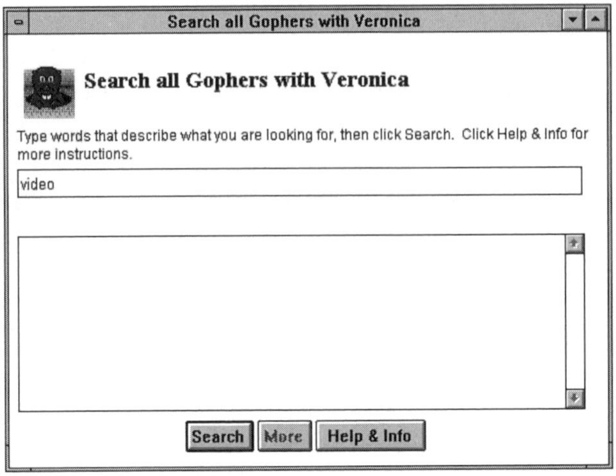

Fig. 12.5
AOL's Veronica search
is one way to find
things that aren't listed
in AOL's categories.

CompuServe

With their new NetLauncher software for Windows, CompuServe has essentially become an Internet Service Provider. **NetLauncher** is a program that dials out and makes the Internet connection. You can access the Internet with any of Windows' Gopher software described in this book (WSGopher or any others from Appendix A, "Other Gopher Software").

You can download CompuServe's NetLauncher package from its Internet window. Or you can call CompuServe at 800-847-0453 to get an evaluation copy.

You access the Internet window from CompuServe's main window, which you see when you log on to CompuServe with WinCim 1.4 (see fig. 12.6).

From here, click the Internet button. If the Internet button doesn't appear on your Browse screen, click the Go button, type **internet**, and click OK. The CompuServe Internet Services window opens, as shown in figure 12.7.

Fig. 12.6
Internet is one of
CompuServe's many
choices. Just click and
go.

Click here for
the Internet

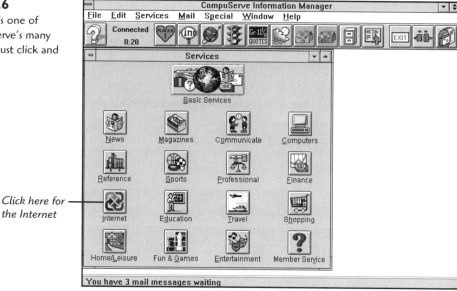

Fig. 12.7
From this window you
can access UseNet
news, FTP, and Telnet.
But to really get
gophering, download
NetLauncher through
the Direct Internet
Access file.

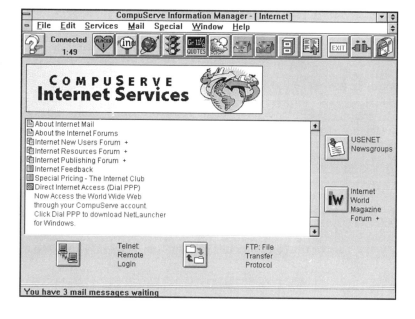

When you click on Direct Internet Access (Dial PPP), WinCim displays a Dialup PPP Window. From here, select NetLauncher for Windows. This opens a window where you can download the 1.2MB NetLauncher file CNL.EXE, and get installation and other information.

 (Tip)

> You may not have to download NetLauncher. If you got CompuServe evaluation disks with a new modem or PC, these disks may already have NetLauncher on them. All you need to do is install it.

The download may take some time, but the installation is fairly easy. Just double-click CNL.EXE in File Manager, the files will self-extract, and the installer program will launch. The installer will prompt you with a series of questions through the NetLauncher installation.

After you download and install NetLauncher, you have access to the Internet through a CompuServe dial-up PPP account. The main software included with NetLauncher is Spry Mosaic, a Web browser, but you can run any Windows Internet software (like WSGopher) with this connection. See Appendix B, "Understanding Internet Connections," for more information.

Plain English, please!

PPP stands for Point-to-Point Protocol. It's one of the ways you can connect to the Internet over a phone line. See Appendix B, "Understanding Internet Connections," for more information. **99**

Because NetLauncher allows you to set up a PPP Internet service account instead of just access to CompuServe's online service, you can run other Internet software across that connection. For example, WSGopher will run over the NetLauncher connection, just as it runs with any other Internet account.

If you've installed NetLauncher, all you need to do is launch your Internet software, like WSGopher, and NetLauncher will start up automatically and make the connection. Then the Internet software uses that connection.

Prodigy

Prodigy allows you to access Gopherspace via the Web, but it does not provide a standard PPP connection. Unlike CompuServe, you can't run other Windows Internet software with Prodigy's Web connection.

To get onto the Internet with Prodigy, launch the Prodigy software for Windows. If you need to get the Prodigy software, call 800-776-3449.

After you're logged into the main Prodigy menu page, select the Web icon from along the bottom of the window. Prodigy then displays the Web menu page, shown in figure 12.8.

Fig. 12.8

After several disclaimers about possible Internet content, Prodigy provides you with access to Gopher via the Web.

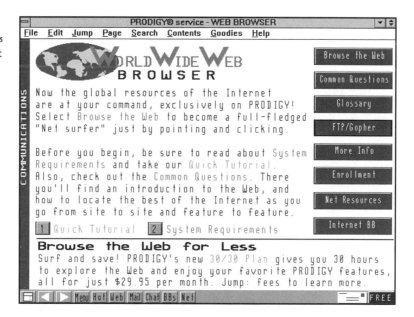

Click Browse the Web to launch the Prodigy browser or click the FTP/Gopher button for information about using the Prodigy browser with Gopher. Clicking the FTP/Gopher button displays a text file that has a couple of sample Gopher addresses.

To get to a Gopher site, you use the Prodigy Web browser. After you've launched the Prodigy Web browser, you can enter a Gopher address, like **gopher://gopher.micro.umn.edu** in the Document URL text box. Figure 12.9

shows the Prodigy browser connected to the server at the University of Minnesota.

Fig. 12.9
You can use this Gopher address, or any other Gopher address, to start searching with Prodigy's Web browser. (See Chapter 14, "Listing of Gopher Sites," for more addresses you can try.)

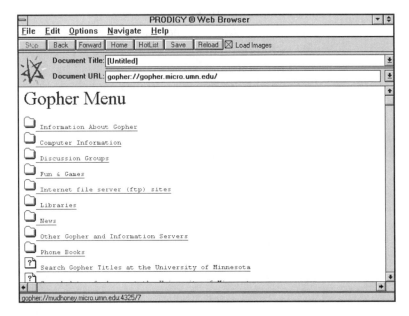

You may recall that the University of Minnesota Gopher has a directory of links to other Gophers. This makes it a good starting place because after you're there you can point and click. After you've found some Gopher starting places with Prodigy's browser, you can save them in a hotlist of Gopher sites.

 Plain English, please!

A **hotlist** is the World Wide Web's equivalent to a list of bookmarks. It's a way to save your place and get back to sites easily and quickly.

One nice feature of Prodigy's browser is that you can create separate hotlists. For example, you could create a hotlist called Gophers, and keep connections to your favorite sites there. Choose Navigate, Hot Lists, and then click Create List. Enter the Hot List name in the dialog box as shown in figure 12.10.

Fig. 12.10
Prodigy's browser
makes it easy to find a
Gopher in the Web.

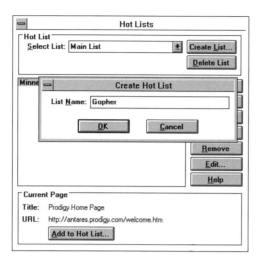

---

①(Tip)

Prodigy's Web access is an additional cost feature. Time is money. You can run
their Web browser without loading graphics to make it run faster with your
connection.

Pipeline

The Pipeline is an online service that's really based on a sort of
"SuperGopher" model. To get an evaluation copy of Pipeline software,
call 800-453-PIPE.

The main Pipeline window, shown in figure 12.11, is basically a Gopher menu
with buttons on the side that launch Web, mail, and other Internet services.

To begin gophering with Pipeline, you can simply point and click and the
next Gopher menu opens, like in figure 12.12. You can also enter Gopher
addresses directly by choosing Internet, Gopher Anywhere. This menu option
lets you enter a Gopher address in a dialog box and go from there.

Fig. 12.11

Pipeline has an all-in-one interface to the Net, built around Gopher menus.

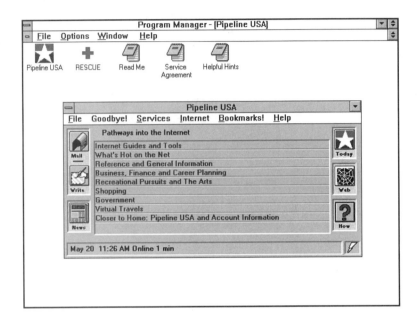

Fig. 12.12

After you start opening windows, Pipeline looks like other Gophers, displaying each new directory in a new window.

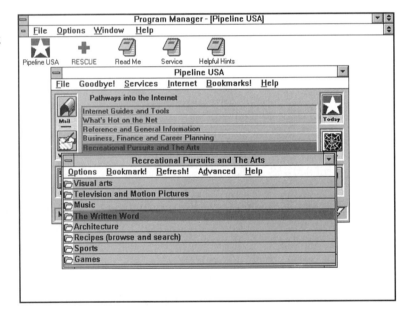

After you're off and gophering with Pipeline, you can save your place with bookmarks. Select an item on a Pipeline menu and click the Bookmark! menu item. Then, from the main Pipeline window, you can select Bookmarks!

to display all the places you have saved. Figure 12.13 shows Pipeline's Bookmarks window.

Fig. 12.13

Pipeline gives you a single bookmark that lists the Internet sites you want to visit again. Items are listed in the order you added them.

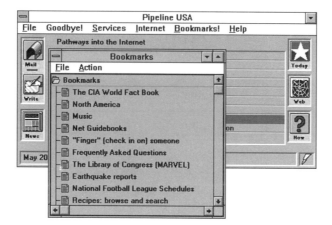

Other online services

Online services like Delphi, GEnie, and any new services that spring up, may give you access to Gopher as part of their Internet connection. This access could be through a Web browser, or some sort of Gopher menu software that looks like other Gophers you're familiar with.

Each of these tools may look slightly different on the surface. But, remember, if it's Gopher, it's a menu-based system that retrieves directories and files. You should be able to burrow right in and begin exploring.

Gophering from the World Wide Web

In this chapter:

- There's a Gopher in the Web
- How to get to Gopherspace with a Web browser
- What does Web software look like in Gopherspace?

Not only can you cruise the Web with your Web browser, you can also search Gopherspace.

E ven though it's the newest part of the Internet, the World Wide Web gives you access to most of Gopherspace, so you can get twice as much information with the same piece of software. Imagine the hassle of switching from one application to another every time you wanted to access these different parts of the Internet. Don't you think it would be easier to access it from the same application? We thought so.

How the WWW connects to Gopherspace

The World Wide Web is the newest, and many think the easiest, way to access the Internet. The Web operates using hypertext, and began at the CERN research center in Switzerland, where physicists created a way to share information, such as graphics, text, and sound, in a more interactive and free-flowing way. They quickly realized that the system they developed translated easily to the Internet, and the Web was up and running.

Plain English, please!

Hypertext is a system whereby many different resources can be linked interactively. The Web makes use of hypertext by a series of HTML (HyperText Markup Language) documents. These documents provide the framework for viewing all kinds of files. The WSGopher Help file, and any other Windows Help file, are examples of hypertext. You can click on certain words in a Help topic that connect you to another topic. With the Web, you can instantly be linked to graphics, sounds, text, and other files found on the Internet.

The software used to navigate the Web is called a browser. Web browsers were originally only text-based. Some programmers at the National Center for Supercomputing Applications (NCSA) soon changed that. They wrote Mosaic, the first Web browser to display text and graphics on the same page.

Because the links to other resources on the Internet are embedded right in the documents, using the Web is like jumping to another Gopher directory from within a Gopher text file instead of having to go back to the Gopher menus to navigate.

With most current Web software, you can also view text and graphics on the same page, and either text or graphics can be links that lead to other locations on the Web. This offers a great advantage in that the Web is much less linear than Gopherspace.

The Web also encompasses other parts of the Internet besides Gopher. From the Web you can access FTP sites, launch Telnet sessions, read newsgroups, and more. Let's take a closer look at how the Web works with Gopher.

How to spot a Gopher on the Web

Because the Web was created only recently, it is able to encompass many of the other Internet protocols, such as FTP, news, and Gopher. You can access Gopher directories with any Web client, either by entering a specific address or just by clicking a link that leads to Gopherspace. You don't need to specifically configure a Web client to read Gopher files, Gopher is just part of the Web.

Because of the way Gopherspace is formatted with menus of directories and files, you can tell if a particular Web site is also a Gopher site by the look of the page. But the real clue is in the address.

Introducing URLs

You've seen what a Gopher address looks like from the introduction to them in Chapter 5, "Using Bookmarks to Save Your Place." If you want a reminder, follow these steps:

1 Open WSGopher.

2 Select any Gopher item.

3 Click the Item Information button.

You'll see a dialog box like the one shown in figure 13.1. This information makes up the Gopher address of the Gopher server at the University of Minnesota, the Mother Gopher.

Fig. 13.1

A Gopher address has many parts, such as the Name, Type, Port, Path, and Host. The Web makes use of a Gopher site's URL.

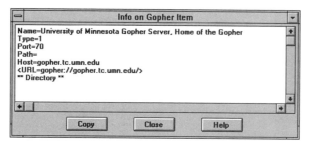

Addresses on the World Wide Web are formatted differently, though they contain much of the same information. A Web address is called a URL, sometimes pronounced "earl," but usually referred to by its initials U-R-L.

Plain English, please!

A **URL** (**Universal Resource Locator**) is an Internet address to one of the protocols reachable through the World Wide Web. A URL is made up of two parts, the protocol and the address, which can often contain a directory path, as well. URLs are generally laid out like this:

protocol://address.of.the.web.page/directory

The first part, *protocol://*, tells the browser what part of the Internet this address is for. The second part, *address.of.the.web.page*, is the Internet address of that item, and */directory* indicates what path to take to get to the desired location.

Gopher URLs

Gopher URLs can get fairly complex because they list the directories and eventually the filename of a Gopher item. Let's start by looking at a simple one: The University of Minnesota:

gopher://gopher.tc.umn.edu/

On a URL with no directory, the final **/** is optional. Most Web browsers will find the site whether you include it or not.

Pretty straightforward, don't you think? Of course, if you want to enter a URL for a Gopher item that's several levels down in a directory tree, it will have a longer URL.

For instance, let's say that you went to the Campus News section of the U of M Gopher. The URL would then look like this:

gopher://gopher.tc.umn.edu:70/11/News

Notice that it now includes a directory path at the end of the host name. This tells your Web browser exactly where to go within that Gopher in order to find the news.

Travel Gopherspace with a Web browser

Getting to Gopherspace with a Web browser can be as easy as entering a Gopher address in an Open URL dialog box. Figures 13.2 and 13.3 show examples of what you can put in such a dialog box using Netscape and where it will take you.

Fig. 13.2
This Open Location dialog box will look different depending on what browser and version you use.

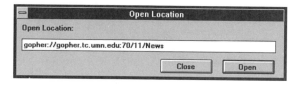

Fig. 13.3
This is where the above URL takes you using a Web browser such as Netscape.

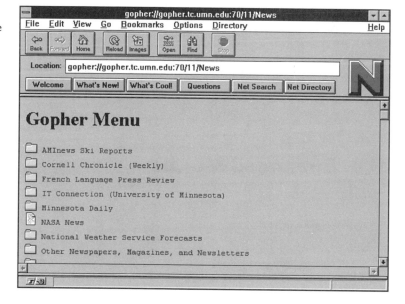

You'll find that you won't have to directly enter a Gopher's URL. Many Web sites provide links to Gopher sites. Because much of the information on Gopher is still useful and current, many Web sites will simply point to the information instead of recreating it as a Web site. To get to these Gopher sites, simply click on the provided link (see fig. 13.4).

No matter which software you use to search the World Wide Web, Gopher appears pretty much as it always does: as a list of menu choices that represent either directories or files. Each Gopher item on the Web page is a link to that directory or file. Point and click and you're navigating Gopherspace as part of the World Wide Web. The figures that follow show what the Mother Gopher looks like in several popular Web browsers.

Fig. 13.4
This Web page at the University of Minnesota provides a direct link to its Gopher site.

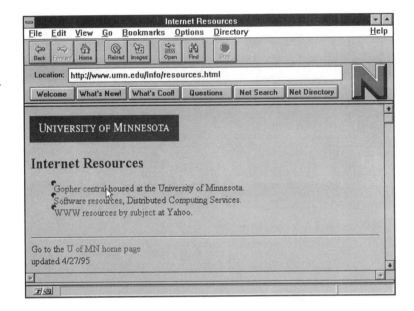

Enhanced Mosaic

Spyglass, Inc.

(708) 505-1010

sales@spyglass.com

http://www.spyglass.com/

Enhanced Mosaic comes from Spyglass and is incorporated into a number of Internet products, from books to integrated Internet software suites. Spyglass is the exclusive licensee of the Mosaic trademark from the University of Illinois. They've rewritten the code for use as a commercial product and licensed and distributed it worldwide.

Figure 13.5 shows a version of Enhanced Mosaic. Various versions of Enhanced Mosaic may have a slightly different look or various custom menus, but they'll have basically the same features and commands.

Fig. 13.5

Spyglass' Enhanced Mosaic will appear slightly different, depending on the books or software package you get it with.

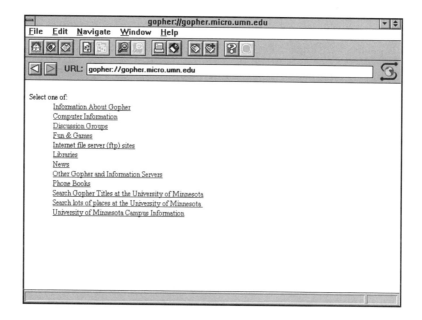

Enhanced Mosaic is available in a number of commercial Internet software packages. It's also included on diskette or CD with several books on the Internet. Look for it at your nearby bookstore or computer retail outlet.

NCSA Mosaic

National Center for Supercomputing Applications

(217) 244-0645

mosaic-w@ncsa.uiuc.edu

ftp://ftp.ncsa.uiuc.edu/Mosaic/Windows/

NCSA Mosaic, shown in figure 13.6, is the forefather of all graphical Web browsers. Since its release in 1993, it has spread across the Net. The interface is updated more quickly and features are added without the longer development cycle demanded by commercial software.

Because it's free from the Net and distributed by the University of Illinois, you can obtain some support for it by contacting their Web page at **http://www.ncsa.uiuc.edu/SDG/Software/WinMosaic/ HomePage.html**. There are also other places to go for help

such as the WWW-related newsgroups, for example
comp.infosystems.www.browsers.ms-windows.

Fig. 13.6

The latest version of NCSA's Mosaic, at the time this book was written. They may have released new versions by now.

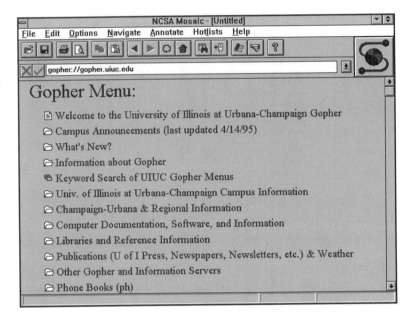

Netscape Navigator

Netscape, Inc.

(415) 528-2555

info@netscape.com

ftp://ftp.netscapc.com/netscape1.1/windows/

The Netscape browser is free from the Net for evaluation purposes. Users at non-educational sites are supposed to register their copies and pay $39.95.

Netscape has been available via FTP and the Web since the fall of 1994, so plenty of people have grabbed a copy. In fact, it has become the most popular Web browser on the market today. It provides an easy-to-use interface and extensive online support (see fig. 13.7).

Fig. 13.7
Netscape, version 1.1N, connected to the Gopher server at Stanford University.

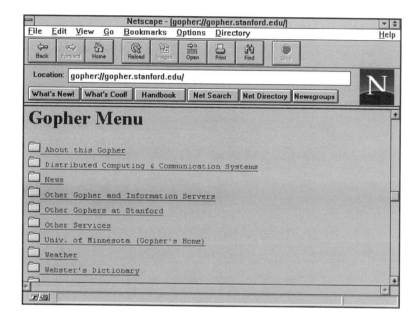

Any browser for the World Wide Web lets you search Gopherspace. Providing access to the various parts of the Internet is one of the Web's biggest strengths. But if you are primarily interested in searching Gopherspace, you may find that a browser like Mosaic or Netscape is simply overkill.

The right tool for the right job

A good Gopher client, like WSGopher, or any of those described in this chapter, requires less memory to run than a Web browser. Gopher clients probably perform faster over a typical dial-up connection as well. For these reasons alone, WSGopher remains a useful tool for Internet searching and file retrieval. Especially if what you're looking for is in Gopherspace.

Part V:

Finding Cool and Useful Gophers

14

Listing of Gopher Sites

In this chapter:

- Gophers for games, recipes, jokes, and more
- Gophers for tools, utilities, and other programs
- Gophers for multimedia files
- Gophers for reference materials and education
- Gophers for jobs, classifieds, and hobbies

Whether your passion is pets or politics, there's a Gopher site out there waiting for you.

Gopher lets you transcend both geography and time zones, allowing you to pursue your interests from the comfort of your own home or office—whenever you want. In this chapter, you'll find some fun and interesting Gopher sites that will help you begin your exploration of the Internet. Each site listed in this chapter includes a brief description of the site and the address of the Gopher server.

If you find a site you like, be sure to add it to your bookmark list. You can also use Gopher searching tools like Veronica and Jughead to help you locate even more sites.

Watch out though—Net-surfing is addictive!

Gophers for games, recipes, jokes, and more

Games

Washington University Archive

address: **wuarchive.wustl.edu**

This site has it all—games, graphics, sound files, UseNet news archives, utilities, and some other things you probably don't know you need yet! Here are some of the interesting choices from the main menu—the pub menu is where you'll find many of the games:

Graphics Programs

Multimedia: Audio, Video, and Images

UseNet News Archives

Useful packages running on many different systems

pub

Internet Wiretap

address: **wiretap.spies.com**

Among other things, Internet Wiretap contains some unique games as well as a collection of tricks and cheats for many classic video games (see fig. 14.1). Two of the selections from the main menu lead you to games and information about games. Choose Video Arcade Collectors Archive for tricks and game lists specific to video arcades, or select Wiretap Online Library, then Mass Media, then Games and Video Games for a more general collection.

Fig. 14.1

If you want to journey to Cyberspace, be sure to visit the Internet Wiretap Gopher at **wiretap.spies.com**.

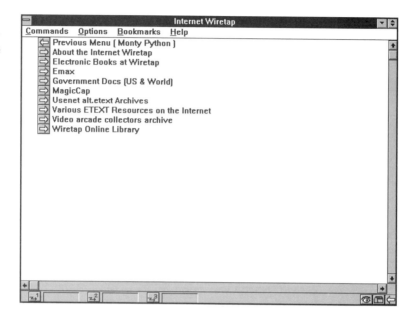

Illuminati Online

address: **pentagon.io.com**

Calling itself, "the online headquarters of the gaming world," Illuminati Online is home to Steve Jackson games, and was once raided by the Secret Service.

University of Minnesota

address: **gopher.tc.umn.edu** or **gopher2.tc.umn.edu**

Frequently called the Mother of all Gopher servers, this site contains, among other things, a collection of games such as Empire of the Petal Throne. From the main menu, choose Fun & Games, then Games.

Recipes

University of Minnesota

address: **ashpool.micro.umn.edu**

If macaroni and cheese doesn't excite you anymore, give the recipes section of this Gopher a try! Included here are recipes for every occasion and every taste. From the main menu, choose Fun, then Recipes.

American Heart Association

address: **gopher.amhrt.org**

If you need information about heart disease, this is the place to look. The American Heart Association Gopher contains lots of statistics on risk factors, support groups, and educational opportunities. To find the section with recipes and cookbooks for healthy hearts, choose Heart Healthy Information from the main menu.

Jokes and more

New Mexico Tech

address: **prism.nmt.edu**

Q: How many software engineers does it take to change a light bulb?

A: None. That's a hardware problem.

The definitive collection of light bulb jokes, as well as thousands of other jokes and humorous anecdotes, can be found at this site. From the main menu, choose Schlake's Humor Archive. Topics are arranged alphabetically.

Camosun College

address: **dragon.camosun.bc.ca**

Monty Python aficionados won't want to miss excerpts from classics like "The Life of Brian," "The Holy Grail," and episodes of the Flying Circus series (see fig. 14.2). You'll also find a great collection of jokes, politically incorrect humor, and Japanese animation. From the main menu, first choose Cybersurfing. Then select Fun Places to Visit, and finally Humour, at which point you'll see these menus:

Monty Python

Humour and Jokes

Comics

Mismash & Politically Incorrect

Fig. 14.2

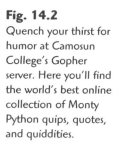

Quench your thirst for humor at Camosun College's Gopher server. Here you'll find the world's best online collection of Monty Python quips, quotes, and quiddities.

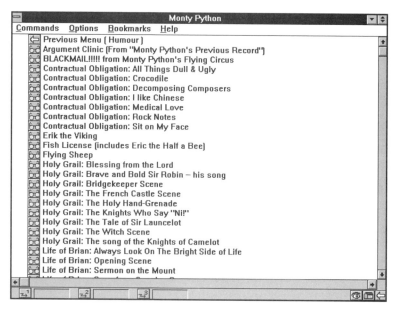

Gophers for tools, utilities, and other programs

Internet tools

University of Minnesota

address: **gopher.tc.umn.edu** or **gopher2.tc.umn.edu**

This is where it all started. University of Minnesota is the home of the original Gopher; and today this site still contains the best collection of Gopher software and information about Gopher, including the annual conference, GopherCON. From the main menu, choose Information about Gopher. Here are some of the menu choices you'll see there:

> About Gopher
>
> Gopher News Archive
>
> Gopher Software Distribution
>
> Commercial Gopher Software
>
> Gopher Protocol Information
>
> University of Minnesota Gopher software licensing policy
>
> Frequently Asked Questions about Gopher
>
> **comp.infosystems.gopher** (UseNet newsgroup)

McMaster University

address: **gopher.mcmaster.ca**

This is another good site for information about Gopher. At the main menu, choose About Gopher (including Help) and then look at the listed choices. Here are some of the interesting choices from the About Gopher menu:

> Documentation for Gopher Information Providers
>
> Frequently Asked Questions About Gopher

Gopher Copyright information

Gopher Jewels

Gopher Training

What is Gopher?

RiceInfo

address: **riceinfo.rice.edu**

Rice University maintains one of the nicest sites around. Of particular interest is the menu choice that arranges Gopher sites by interest area from Aerospace to Women and Gender. If you select Information by Subject Area from the main menu, here's just a small sampling of what you'll find:

Architecture

Economics and Business

Film and Television

Music

Oceanography

Travel

Women and Gender

Utilities

CICA (Center for Innovative Computing Applications)

address: **cica-gopher.cica.indiana.edu**

CICA maintains one of the largest collections of Windows and Windows NT software on the Internet. Here you'll find both general and Internet utilities, icons, sound files, PIMs (Personal Information Managers), and hard-to-find hardware drivers. From the main menu, choose CICA PC/Windows

Anonymous FTP Archives, PC and CICA Windows Files, CICA Windows Files. Here are just a few of the menu items you'll find there:

Desktop Utilities

Fonts (Printer and Screen)

Games and Diversions

Icons and Icon-related files

Miscellaneous Windows Files

Sounds and sound utils, wavs

MERIT (University of Michigan)

address: **gopher.archive.merit.edu**

This is a great site for Internet tools and utilities for both MS-DOS and Macintosh, as well as language instruction. From the main menu, choose Merit Software Archives.

Lancaster University (UK)

address: **micros.hensa.ac.uk**

This site is great! It features a Top 50 list of software for DOS, Windows, Macintosh, Amiga, Atari, and others. Whether you're looking for Internet utilities, virus software, screen savers, or a variety of useful tools, you're bound to find it here. To access this huge collection of software, at the main menu select The HENSA/micros archive at Lancaster University. Make note that due to the traffic on this site, it is only available between 8 p.m. and 8 a.m. GMT.

Gopher Jewels™—University of Southern California

address: **cwis.usc.edu**

Gopher Jewels is a catalog of Gopher resources, indexed by topic. Pick from over 20 categories, or perform a Jughead search of all the menus in Gopher Jewels. From the USC main menu, choose Other Gophers and Information

Resources, Gophers by Subject. Figure 14.3 shows what you see when you choose Gopher Jewels.

Fig. 14.3
The Gopher Jewels server at the University of Southern California is an excellent resource for locating other Gopher sites on the Internet. Gopher servers are indexed by subject; or you can perform a Jughead search to locate a particular topic.

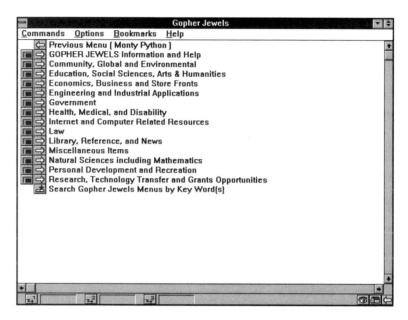

Gophers for multimedia files

Graphics

Exploratorium Gopher

address: **gopher.exploratorium.edu**

The welcome message describes the Exploratorium like this: "The Exploratorium is a museum of science, technology, and human perception located in the Palace of Fine Arts in the Marina district of San Francisco." You won't want to miss the Exploratorium Imagery menu item, where you'll find over two dozen high-quality images of distorted rooms, bubbles, lightning, and other magic.

Smithsonian Institution's National Museum of American Art

address: **nmaa-ryder.si.edu**

What do Mary Cassatt, George Inness, Thomas Hart Benton, Frederick Brown, Georgia O'Keeffe, and Oqwa Pi have in common? They are all American artists whose art is available digitally in the archives of the Smithsonian Institution's National Museum of American Art (see fig. 14.4). This is a wonderful site that contains downloadable images of artwork produced by America's finest painters and sculptors. Search for your favorite artist, or just peruse the collection. Each image is accompanied by text that gives biographical information about the artist.

Fig. 14.4

Classic works of art by America's finest painters and sculptors are available digitally from the Smithsonian Institution's National Museum of American Art.

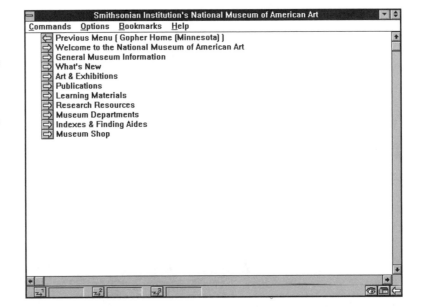

ArchiGopher

address: **libra.arch.umich.edu**

The University of Michigan's doctoral program in architecture has put together a fascinating Gopher that includes images of Wassily Kandinsky paintings, Andrea Palladio's architecture, and architecture from the Hellenic and Byzantine eras. Some of the interesting menus include:

The Kandinsky Image Archive

The Palladio Image Archive

Images of 3D CAD Models

Musings on Lunar Architecture

Greek Architecture

Tunisian Architecture (New)

U.C. Berkeley Museum of Paleontology

address: **ucmp1.berkeley.edu**

You don't have to be a paleontologist to enjoy this fascinating collection of images from the Museum of Paleontology. Explore the natural history exhibits of sharks, dinosaurs, birds, whale sounds, and other images of biological and botanical diversity. From the main menu, choose Natural History Exhibits.

Sound Files

Hearts of Space

address: **hos.com**

Abandoning a career in architecture, Stephen Hill started Music From the Hearts of Space in 1973. Since then, Hearts of Space, featuring a genre of music dubbed "spacemusic," has become the most popular contemporary music program on public radio. Check out these menu items from the main menu:

Almost Everything You Wanted to Know About Hearts of Space

Hearts of Space Radio Playlists

Stations Carrying Hearts of Space Radio

Hearts of Space Records

New Age Music Made Simple, by Stephen Hill

Grateful Dead Gopher

address: **gdead.berkeley.edu**

Serious Deadheads will not want to miss this site! Playlists, lyrics, audio clips, graphics galore, concert schedules, and interviews with Jerry and the gang—it's all here. Some of the items from the main menu include:

drop-box

graphics

interviews

lyrics

sounds

stats

tour_dates

Videos

Internet Wiretap

address: **wiretap.spies.com**

There's something for everyone at Wiretap. Here you'll find a unique collection of videos, games, humor, musical discographies, and other things for nearly every sort of enthusiast. From the main menu, choose Wiretap Online Library, then check out some of these menus:

Cyberspace

Fringes of Reason

Humor

Mass Media

Music

SunSITE (University of North Carolina)

address: **sunsite.unc.edu**

SunSITE is home to OTIS, a collection of original artwork and photographs for public viewing and distribution. While you're here, take some time to explore other menus—this site also has a great collection of animation, music, humor, games, and much, much more. To reach the multimedia section, select Worlds of SunSITE—by Subject from the main menu. From there, choose Browse All SunSITE Archives, then multimedia. Here are some of the selections from that menu:

animation

chinese-music

emusic

pc-sounds

pictures

talk-radio

utilities

Gophers for reference materials and education

Online books

The Gutenberg Project

address: **gopher.etext.org**

The goal of the Gutenberg Project is to provide an electronic collection of 10,000 of the world's most read books by the year 2001. To access the current collection, select Gutenberg from the main menu. This Gopher also maintains an eclectic collection of essays, political treatises, and religious texts. Check out the Anamnesis selection from the Poetry menu for a self-contained multimedia book that combines award-winning sci-fi with sound effects, graphics, and video.

The Online Book Initiative

address: **world.std.com**

The Online Book Initiative is one of several Internet sites that makes available electronic copies of non-copyrighted materials such as books, reference material, and conference proceedings. Here you can find the full text of Shakespearean plays, Mary Shelley's *Frankenstein*, Thomas Paine's *Common Sense*, Grimm's Fairy Tales, the works of Mark Twain, and episodes from *Star Trek*. From the main menu, choose the OBI The Online Book Initiative menu item for an alphabetized list of the holdings.

Articles

The Electronic Newsstand

address: **gopher.enews.com**

The Electronic Newsstand is a place where you can browse through hundreds of publications on topics as diverse as travel, science, business, foreign affairs, the arts, health and nutrition, sports, and, of course, computers. Each Newsstand publisher provides the table of contents and several articles from each current issue. Be sure to read the copyright information, then check out the many publications listed in these menus:

Electronic Bookstore

Electronic Car Showroom

Business and Finance Center

Computers and Technology Resources

Entertainment Area

Health and Medical Center

The Renaissance Room

Sports, Recreation and Leisure Center

The WELL

address: **gopher.well.sf.ca.us**

An offspring of Whole Earth Review and the Whole Earth Catalog, the WELL (Whole Earth Lectronic Link) provides access to tools, ideas, and people. Use the Search menu to look for a particular topic, or browse through these menu items on your own:

Internet Outbound (Links we think are cool)

Art, Music, Film, Cultural works, etc.

Authors, Books, Periodicals, Zines

Business in Cyberspace

Communications and Media

Community

Cyberpunk and Postmodern Culture

Environmental Issues and Ideas

The Military, its People, Policies, and Practices

Whole Earth Review, the Magazine

Whole Systems

Education

The KIDLINK Gopher

address: **kids.duq.edu**

The KIDLINK Gopher is probably the only server of its kind on the Internet. KIDLINK enables kids—ages 10 to 15—to engage in global communication through language learning and direct communication with other kids around the world. Young artists and writers can also submit original computer art, poetry, and compositions for publishing on the server. Check out these menu items:

Finding and Using KIDLINK Services

Special Language KIDLINK Documents and Lists

KIDLINK in the Classrooms

KIDLINK People

KIDART Computer Art Gallery

KIDSHOW and other multimedia programs about KIDLINK

Directly Access the KIDLINK Archive LOG files

U.S. Department of Education Office of Education Research and Improvement

address: **gopher.ed.gov**

If you want to know what the government is doing to improve the quality of education in the U.S., then this is the place to look. This site contains information about primary and secondary education, government goals for the year 2000, and distance learning. The last item on the main menu leads you to some education software that you can download. Here are some of the menu choices:

U.S. Department of Education Programs—General Information

Department-wide Initiatives (Goals 2000...)

Educational Research, Improvement, and Statistics (OERI & NCES)

Elementary and Secondary Education (OESE), and Early Childhood

School-to-Work, Vocational and Adult Education (OVAE)

Announcements, Bulletins, and Press Releases

U.S. Department of Education/OERI Publications

U.S. Department of Education Phone Directory

Education Software

InforMNs

address: **informns.k12.mn.us**

While InforMNs was developed as a way to provide services and tools to Minnesota's K-12 educators, there are numerous menu items of general interest, in particular international expeditions, exchanges, and wildlife research projects. From the main menu, select Best of the K-12 Internet Resources, where you will find these menu items:

Bosnian/Croatian Exchange Projects

Circumpolar Expedition: May 11-18, 1994

Map the Monarchs!

Mayaquest

NASA

Reports from McMurdo Station, Antarctica

Wolf Study Project

Government information

Electronic Government Information Service

address: **eryx.syr.edu**

Want to get the jump on the latest White House press releases? Ever wonder what's in the CIA Fact Book, need access to U.S. Census Data, or want to read Supreme Court decisions? It's all here at the Electronic Government Information Service. This site contains one of the most comprehensive sources of government information as well as connections to some FreeNet accounts. Here are the choices at the main menu:

By Federal Agency

Citizen's Guide to FOIA

City Guides (Freenets)

Court Opinions

Guides

Key Documents

Law School OPACs

NCLIS

Policy Documents

SPIN

Statistics

White House Information

Counterpoint Publishing's Internet Services

address: **gopher.counterpoint.com**

Although Counterpoint is a commercial provider, it has made an outstanding effort to provide government information that is difficult to locate elsewhere. For example, you can find data from the Nuclear Regulatory Commission and the U.S. Department of Energy. According to the Welcome file, Counterpoint provides "the nation's only Internet version of state environmental regulations." Take a look at these menu choices:

United States Federal Register

United States Commerce Business Daily

Code of Federal Regulations

DOE Orders and NRC Regulatory Guides

State Environmental Regulations

Library of Congress

address: **marvel.loc.gov**

You can't download a book from the Library of Congress, but you can use the Library of Congress Information System (LOCIS) free of charge to locate resources in the Library's vast collection. THOMAS, another free service, allows you to search House and Senate bills, or read congressional records. If nothing else, check out the fascinating history of this American institution which boasts collections in over 400 languages and is the national library for the blind and physically handicapped. Here are some choices from the main menu:

Research and Reference (Public Services)

Events, Facilities, Publications, and Services

Copyright

Library of Congress Online Systems

U.S. Congress

Global Electronic Library (by Subject)

U.S. Congress Gopher

address: **gopher.house.gov** or **gopher.senate.gov**

Each house of the U.S. Congress has its own Gopher server which you can browse for committee information, legislature in progress, and the full text of the U.S. Constitution (see fig. 14.5). Many members of Congress have e-mail addresses, and you can find these here as well. The House server even provides a Guest Register—an online form you can fill out to leave comments for your member of Congress.

Fig. 14.5
Many state and federal agencies maintain their own Gopher servers. Both the U.S. Senate, as well as the U.S. House of Representatives, have Gopher servers which you can browse for legislation in progress and where you can find the e-mail addresses of members of Congress.

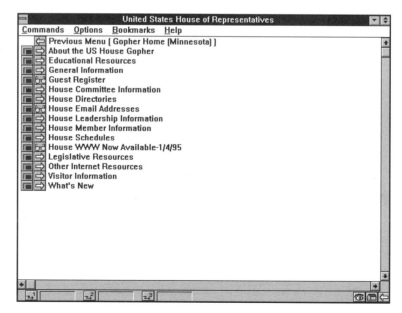

The United Nations

address: **gopher.undp.org**

This site is amazing in its scope and completeness. There are excellent entries on the history of the United Nations, peace-keeping activities, United Nations Children's Fund (UNICEF), Security Council documents, and links to numerous environmental sites. Here's a sampling from the main menu:

The United Nations, what it is and what it does

United Nations Current Information (Highlists, Press Releases, etc.)

United Nations Documents (General Assembly, Sec. Council)

United Nations Conferences

United Nations Economic and Social Council (ECOSOC)

United Nations System Telecommunications Catalogue

Environment Related Information

UseNet news archives

University of Waterloo

address: **watserv2.uwaterloo.ca**

Whether you need help in getting started with UseNet, or just want to browse through the existing UseNet archives, this is a good place to start. From the main menu, choose Electronic Resources Around the World, Guides to Internet Services, and then UseNet—Internet newsgroups. Here you'll find everything you want to know about UseNet:

What is UseNet?

UseNet Software: History and Sources

Emily Postnews Answers Your Questions on Netiquette

UseNet Newuser

UseNet Rules of Conduct

Frequently asked questions (FAQs) archives

UseNet newsgroups archives (WAIS)

University of New Brunswick

address: **jupiter.sun.csd.unb.ca**

This site contains the FAQs (Frequently Asked Questions) from all of the major newsgroups including alt and clari. The main menu option for this is:

UseNet News Frequently Asked Questions... FAQs

Weather maps

The University of Illinois Weather Machine

address: **wx.atmos.uiuc.edu**

The U of I Weather Machine provides up-to-date weather information including forecasts and a variety of satellite images for every state as well as Canada, the Caribbean, and other international locations. Here are some selections from the main menu:

Canada

Caribbean

Case Studies

Images

Latin America

Other Servers

Purdue WXP Gopher

address: **thunder.atms.purdue.edu**

The Purdue WXP Gopher provides surface, upper, radar, and satellite images from the National Weather Service.

Gophers for jobs, classifieds, and hobbies

Job postings

Academic Positions Network (APN)

address: **wcni.cis.umn.edu**

The Academic Positions Network (APN) is a worldwide network for positions in academia. Look here for faculty, staff, and administrative job postings as well as graduate fellowships, assistantships, and post-docs. In addition to menu items for each state and Central America, you'll find these items at the main menu:

> Search for Files
>
> William C. Norris Institute
>
> Placing an Announcement

Dartmouth College

address: **dartcms1.dartmouth.edu**

This site maintains a list of federal job openings and related information. From the main menu, select Job Openings in the Federal Government. From there, you'll see menu items with job announcements, pay-scale information, and helpful hints for federal job applicants. Here are just a few of the menu choices:

> Federal Gov't Position Announcements
>
> Private Industry Position Announcements
>
> Salary Pay Tables for Federal Civilian Emply
>
> Specific Locality Pay Tables for Federal Emply
>
> Federal Job Classification
>
> Federal Group Occupational Requirements
>
> Miscellaneous info useful to job applicants

Chronicle of Higher Education

address: **chronicle.merit.edu**

If you're job hunting, be sure to take a look at the Chronicle of Higher Education's current job postings. In addition to academic positions, there are job offerings covering a wide range of occupations from art galleries to environmental groups to medical facilities. From the main menu, choose Jobs In and Out of Academe. You can then search for jobs in a variety of pre-selected areas, or do a keyword search.

Massachusetts Institute of Technology (MIT)

address: **marathon.mit.edu**

MIT's personnel office posts full- and part-time listings for technical, administrative, and library positions. From the main menu, select MIT TechInfo, Jobs and Volunteer Opportunities, then Personnel Office Job listing.

Academic Physician and Scientist

address: **acad-phy-sci.com**

This is a comprehensive resource that advertises positions in academic medicine. You may also subscribe to this service and receive free bi-monthly updates. Here are the main menu choices:

About Academic Physician and Scientist

Contacts at Academic Physician and Scientist

Administrative Positions

Basic Science Positions

Clinical Science Positions

Food and Drug Administration (FDA) Opportunities

NIH Opportunities

For sale/Want to buy

The Human Factor

address: **people.human.com**

This site is home to a couple of interesting Internet gems, including RadioNet Interactive Radio, and *FOR SALE BY OWNER* magazine, which contains classified ads for buying and selling property. (Although not restricted geographically, most listings tend to be in California.) Choose FOR SALE BY OWNER from the main menu.

Texas Metronet

address: **gopher.metronet.com**

Hundreds of computer and software companies submit new product announcements to the **comp.newprod** UseNet newsgroup. You don't have to read UseNet news to find out about new products—you can find them all here in this searchable archive which is also organized by vendor and month. From the main menu, select the comp.newprod archives.

Sample hobby sites

University of Colorado, Boulder

address: **culine.colorado.edu**

Professional sports enthusiasts can keep up to date, by viewing online the schedules of some of their favorites sports leagues. Choose Professional Sports Schedules from the main menu to view these items:

> Australian Football League
>
> Canadian Football League
>
> National Football League
>
> American Hockey League

National Basketball Association

Major League Baseball

Moon Travel Handbooks

address: **gopher.moon.com**

If you find yourself drawn to Indonesia and the South Pacific, Europe, South America, or Africa, you'll probably want to do some armchair exploring beforehand at the Moon Travel Handbooks Gopher. According to the welcome message, "Moon Publications has produced travel handbooks that are both cultural essays and consumer reports." Here you'll also find an interactive journey across the U.S., called Road Trip U.S.A. From the main menu, select Moon Travel Handbooks to view these selections:

About Moon Travel Handbooks

Search titles of all files and menus

Road Trip USA

Trans-Cultural Study Guide

Asia Travel Booklists

Travel Health: Staying Healthy in Asia, Africa, and Latin America

Travel Matters Newsletter (free subscription)

Catalog of Moon Travel Handbooks

Ordering Information

VeloNet—The Global Cycling Network

address: **cycling.org**

If you are a cycling enthusiast, this site is a must! VeloNet is an information desk for cyclists, with listings of bicycling organizations, contacts, and ride schedules around the globe (see fig. 14.6). The Reading Room menu item contains a wealth of information about biking safety, health and fitness, mountain biking, cycling events for the disabled, and much, much more.

Fig. 14.6

Whether your passion is skydiving or horticulture, nearly every hobby is represented by a site on the Internet, including this Gopher server for VeloNet, the Global Cycling Network.

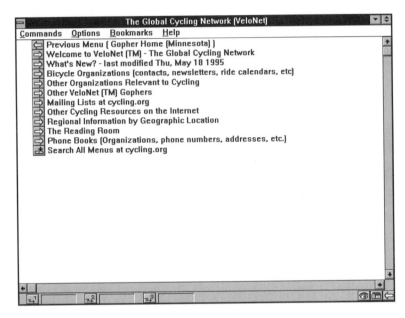

Texas Agricultural Extension

address: **leviathan.tamu.edu**

A rose by any other name might smell as sweet, but if you want to know how to care for cannas, daylilies, and a garden full of other perennials, annuals, vegetables, and shrubs, you'll want to come to this site. From the main menu, select Master Gardener Information. From here, locate your favorite gardening topic from among these menu choices:

Full text search of Master Gardener Menus

Full text search of Master Gardener Files

Fruits and Nuts

Flowering Plants, Annual and Perennial

Ornamental Trees and Shrubs

Turf Grasses

Vegetables

Texas A&M University

address: **gopher.cs.tamu.edu**

If you're a ham radio operator, you may be interested in this site. From the main menu, select Access to TAMU Anonymous FTP file, then ham radio.

The Internet Hunt—in a class by itself

Here's a site that doesn't fit any category. It's an Internet scavenger hunt for facts and trivia on the Internet. Here's how the hunt works: each month, twelve questions are posed that challenge you to find a particular site on the Internet. The first person or team to submit the correct answers wins fame and even a few prizes! To reach the hunt, select The Internet Hunt from the main menu.

Internet Hunt—CICnet
address: **gopher.cic.net**

Part VI:

Gopher and Beyond

Chapter 15: The Future of Gopher

15 The Future of Gopher

With competitors like the World Wide Web and Mosaic, how will Gopher continue to be a significant Internet resource?

In this chapter:

- What's the future look like for Gopher?
- Can Gopher survive in tomorrow's Internet?
- Some new ideas about using Gopher

I s Gopher becoming extinct? Is it destined to go the way of the dinosaurs, fading in the wake of Mosaic's meteoric popularity? It's hard to believe that in 1990 there was no such thing as Gopher. Soon after its development in 1991, Gopher enjoyed an exponential growth in popularity and it had only one major competitor.

Gopher's competition only had a real advantage on expensive graphical computer systems where you could display pictures and text together on one screen. That competitor was the World Wide Web; and a program called Mosaic has recently altered the landscape considerably. Now, thanks to inexpensive and powerful computer hardware, everybody can use a graphical environment, such as Windows, Mac OS, and OS/2. The Web has gained new stature within the online world. What's the future of Gopher in this new landscape?

Gopher's place on the Internet landscape

The complete extinction of Gopher is not likely, because Gopher servers' ability to organize information and manage data make them an attractive target even for these new Web browsers. But Gopher clients seem to be in jeopardy. The ease with which newer programs such as Mosaic and Netscape can access Gopher servers might check the growth of Gopher as an Internet service with its own identity.

Some new ideas in using Gopher might be the key to keeping the Gopher service viable. There are a couple of interesting prospects, and in this chapter we'll see how they bring some fresh concepts to the use of an Internet resource that, by now, we've not only gotten quite used to but grown quite fond of as well.

Some new ideas on the horizon

Several new Gopher clients and interfaces have appeared recently that may change the thinking about how we use Gopher. Some innovative concepts have been applied to using a very traditional kind of Gopher service.

Gophermoo: Gopher in virtual reality

Gophermoo is based on a game technology that's been around the Internet for a number of years. You may have heard of the fantasy game Dungeons and Dragons, in which players control the actions of a character in a made-up world. The online version of this concept is called a MUD, for Multi-User Dungeon. A MUD allows multiple people to participate in an online game usually done over the Internet.

Gophermoo is a new kind of server that creates a text-based virtual reality and allows you to use items in Gopherspace as if you were in real space. The "moo" in Gophermoo stands for Mud Object Oriented. Gophermoo creates a space in which Gopher items exist as objects within a room. You can visit that room, collect objects (Gopher menus you've visited), leave the room, and come back to it in the same state that you left it. Because Gophermoo is a multi-user server, someone else might be in the room with you and you can collaborate on some Internet exploration.

Plain English, please!

Virtual reality is an environment simulated by a computer. For many years, novels have been the best examples of virtual reality. They create a world which is similar to the one we know, but can include characters, events, and places which we ordinarily wouldn't be able to experience. Computers are becoming even better at creating these kinds of environments which let us travel to places ordinarily inaccessible.

A taste of Gophermoo is given in the following section, which takes you through a Gophermoo session. The text of this online session almost reads like a story. While there are other characters present during the following exploratory session, you don't interact with them. But one of the strengths of this environment is that you can share what you find with someone else who is visiting the virtual world.

You can try out Gophermoo by selecting <u>N</u>ew Gopher Item from the WSGopher <u>F</u>ile menu.

1 In the Server Name text box, type **jayshouse.ccs.neu.edu**.

2 In the port text box, type **1709**.

3 Use the pull-down menu to select Telnet in the Item Type menu.

Press Enter or click on OK and WSGopher will open a Telnet session to the Gophermoo server. Type **connect guest** and when you get a `*connected*` message you can start exploring. You can navigate through the online environment by entering directional commands like, up, down, north, south, east, and west.

```
*** Connected ***

Underground

This is a dark, cramped space. It appears to be very crowded in
here; you keep bumping into what feels like drainage pipes, alli-
gators, and other people (apparently sleeping). One useful thing
that you've discovered in your bumbling about is a manhole cover
above you.
```

```
* Welcome to JHM.                              *

* As it says above, this is not a game, and people here will
take  *

* your actions seriously. Type:                    *

*  help manners - to learn about the standards of behavior here
*

*  @911 <your question>  - if you require emergency assistance
*

*  @tutorial  - to learn how to use MOO.              *

*                              *

* Note that other users of this MOO will be able to tell where
you  *

* have connected from.                       *
```

There is new news. Type 'news' to read all news or 'news new' to
read just new news.

As you can see, our entry into this world is underground and the best place to
go is up. You can type the command **up** to move above ground.

>up

You push the manhole cover aside and squint in the light...

Hwy. 169

A swath of blacktop scything through the forest to the west and
farmland to the east. Trucks rumble past, accelerated to dangerous
speeds by wild-eyed drivers on dangerous amphetamines; cars scream
past as well, most piloted by alcohol-mad college students driven
over the edge by one too many calculus midterms. This is a dangerous place to be.

A small driveway dips into the woods to the west here, and you
notice (strangely enough) a manhole cover in the middle of the
highway.

rocker and Pyrobyr are here, off in another world.

Above ground, we can start moving toward Jay's house, where we will find
Gopher items. The characters rocker and Pyrobyr represent other users of
the Jayshouse computer, but they are not in the immediate vicinity of this
virtual landscape. We can enter the command, **west**, until we get to the patio
of Jay's house. After we enter the house, we can explore until we find the
library which contains the Gopher resources.

The West Patio

You're standing on the western part of the patio. To the north is
the first floor wall of the house; windows look in on two rooms.
The second story deck projects from the house over part of the
patio, providing shelter and shade. There's a door into the house
in the middle of the wall. The ledge of a low concrete wall continues here from the east; past it is a lawn and garden area which
drops off quickly to the creekbed. A folding couch is here. A
narrow path into the woods to the south leads down to a small
footbridge crossing the creek.

>**north**

You open the door and walk into the house.

Jay's Room

What a mess! Papers, books, gadgets, clothes and silly things
cover the floor of this room to mid-calf level. One would suspect
that there's a thriving micro-ecology in here. A bed is against
the south wall, but it's half-covered in more junk. There's an IBM
PC on a bad computer desk in one corner, and lots of things connected together with alligator clips are hooked up to it. On the
east wall is yellow wallpaper featuring smiling dinosaurs. To the
south is also a door to the outside. North is the door into the
rest of the house.

Tari is here, off in another world. Jay is asleep.

>**north**

You leave Jay's room finally.

The Downstairs Hallway

You are in a small hallway that connects the five downstairs
rooms. To the west, a vinyl folding door opens on a small storeroom. A closed dark wooden door on the south wall stands
uninvitingly closed. Towards the east end of the south wall is a
open door to the master bedroom. To the east is the laundry room,
and on the north is the closed door to the bathroom. Broad stairs
lead up to the second floor. The vinyl door to the storeroom is
open. The bathroom door to the bathroom is open. The master bedroom door to the master bedroom is open.

You see a flat-top trunk and a round-top trunk here.

Joe is here, daydreaming.

>**up**

You walk up the stairs.

The Upstairs Hallway

You're in the hallway landing that looks over the staircase. It's
lit by an odd hanging light fixture. At the east end of the open
hallway is the dining room. The library entrance is to the west;
nearby on the south wall is the door to Nell's bedroom.

Juggler is here, dozing.

>**west**

The Library

The library is a fairly small room lit by a single plain fixture
in the center of the ceiling. The room is roughly rectangular. A
single huge oak bookcase stands against the northern wall. An oak
table is here. A basket of blank nametags is here. A wooden door
with a small lighted sign reading 'EXIT' above it leads east.

You see a slate dispenser, a treasure hunt, the feature object
registry, a large box of radios, and the library's slate here.

>look at library's slate

Slate

A laptop size computer, with various controls on it.

   1. The U of I Weather Machine (menu)

   2. Lyrics directory (menu)

   3. recipes WAIS search (search)

   4. Electronic Frontier Foundation archives (menu)

   5. Dictionary (sound-like) search (search)

   6. Movie reviews (menu)

>pick 1 on slate

You pick '1. The U of I Weather Machine (menu)' on the library's
slate.

   1. :NOTICE: Satellite products unavailable

   2. :The UofI Weather Machine

   3. Canada (menu)

   4. Caribbean (menu)

   5. Case Studies (menu)

   6. Documents (menu)

   7. Illinois (menu)

8. Images (menu)

9. International (menu)

10. Latin America (menu)

11. Other Servers (menu)

12. Regional (menu)

13. Satellite Discussion (menu)

14. Severe (menu)

15. States (menu)

>pick 15 on slate

You pick '15. States (menu)' on the library's slate.

1. Alabama (menu)

2. Alaska (menu)

3. Arizona (menu)

4. Arkansas (menu)

5. California (menu)

6. Colorado (menu)

7. Connecticut (menu)

---- 'next on slate' to see additional choices (51 total) ---

>pick 5 on slate

You pick '5. California (menu)' on the library's slate.

1. Ag Fcst (Bakersfield)

2. Ag Fcst (Fresno)

3. Ag Fcst (Sacramento-SAC)

4. Ag Fcst (Santa Maria)

5. Ag and Frost Fcst (Chico)

```
 6. Ag and Frost Fcst (Imperial)

 7. Ag and Frost Fcst (Palm Springs)

 8. Ag and Frost Fcst (Ukiah)

 9. Agri Advisory (50)

10. Climatology Report Daily (Bakersfield)

11. Climatology Report Daily (Eureka-EKA)

12. Climatology Report Daily (Fresno)

13. Climatology Report Daily (Los Angeles)

14. Climatology Report Daily (Redding)

15. Climatology Report Daily (Sacramento-SAC)

16. Climatology Report Daily (San Diego-SAN)

17. Climatology Report Daily (San Francisco-SFO)

---- 'next on slate' to see additional choices (78 total) ---
```

When you pick 17, you get the National Weather Service's daily climatological report for the San Francisco-SFO area. This report outlines, in table format, the daily temperature highs, lows, and records set.

At this point you could look at more items on the slate, explore other parts of the house, or type @quit to exit the jayshouse computer.

If you want to learn more about Gophermoo, visit the anonymous FTP site, **parcftp.xerox.com**, and browse the /pub/MOO directory.

Gophermoo is somewhat limited by its text interface, but not because you have to imagine the surroundings (although a generation raised on TV might have trouble with that). Gophermoo is controlled by commands typed in at the keyboard. This is not the most natural way for people to navigate through an unknown landscape. Still, the concepts behind Gophermoo are quite creative and may inspire some further developments along this line.

TurboGopher VR

GopherVR takes the concept of virtual reality one step further by using three-dimensional graphic images to create a small landscape that can be navigated by literally moving in one direction or another. Currently there are two versions available for only two kinds of computer systems (UNIX and Macintosh) and the software is experimental.

You can see an example of GopherVR in figure 15.1. This is the initial screen that you see when you run TurboGopherVR, the Macintosh version of GopherVR. You can move to the right around this circle by pressing the mouse button and moving the mouse to the right. You want to move left? Press the mouse button and move your mouse to the left. Moving the mouse up moves you forward and close to one of the monoliths. Moving the mouse down moves you backward.

When you click on one of the menu items you will be taken to the new menu. (You will actually start from an aerial view and fly down to a new set of monoliths.) Currently, the same scene is used for all menus, but the developers of GopherVR have imagined a version for which Gopher system managers could create their own three-dimensional scenes and allow people to navigate among various items.

Fig. 15.1

A virtual reality version of Gopher provides a more intuitive method to navigate Gopherspace.

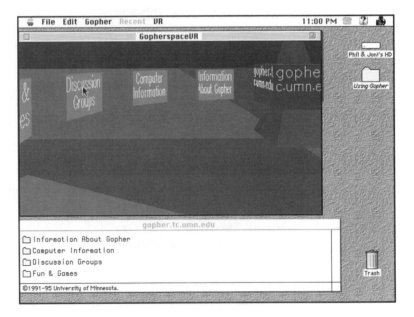

TurboGopherVR currently only runs on a Power Macintosh running System 7 or greater (system 7.5.1 is recommended). You can download the program by visiting the Gopher, **boombox.micro.umn.edu**, and looking in the /gopher/ Macintosh-TurboGopher/TurboGopherVR menu path. There is also GopherVR version for X windows running on a UNIX system (several different types of Unix systems are supported). You'll find the UNIX versions on the boombox Gopher in the gopher/Unix/GopherVR menu path. No Windows version is available as of this writing, but if the virtual reality Gopher catches on, it won't be long until it inhabits all kinds of computers. Watch for the Windows version to show up on the boombox Gopher.

Blue Skies

Sometimes people can find a creative new way to use an existing technology. This is the case with Blue Skies Gopher. Blue Skies is a program that adapts Gopher's information retrieval capability to the task of providing up-to-date graphically oriented weather information to people on the Internet. Blue Skies is copyrighted, but freely usable, software that is available on the Internet.

Blue Skies extends the capabilities of Gopher to include the display of some high-quality graphic images. One special feature is its ability to use interactive weather maps—if you want to know the temperature in Cleveland, you just click on Cleveland. When you start up Blue Skies, instead of the normal Gopher menu, you see a series of pictures which represent information or files available from the Internet. You can see the opening screen of Blue Skies in figure 15.2.

As shown in figure 15.3, you can click on the weather map to bring up a menu of interactive weather maps. This is actually a Gopher menu, but the features of the Gopher client are somewhat enhanced (the little triangles let you display the next menu level within the same screen).

You can double-click on one of the listed titles and a weather map with some commentary is displayed. On the Interactive Weather Map, you can click on one of the city locations represented by a pink dot, and see the weather conditions at that location. Figure 15.4 shows what a typical weather map looks like.

Fig. 15.2
Blue Skies Gopher
extends the capabilities
of a traditional Gopher
client.

Fig. 15.3
Blue Skies shows a
Gopher menu of
weather maps that
you can use to find
weather information.

You can also access the normal Gopher resources with Blue Skies, including
the University of Minnesota Gopher. In Blue Skies, however, Gopher is called
Groundhog (the same as a gopher, but more related to weather, I guess).
Clicking on the picture of the groundhog at the computer terminal seen in
figure 15.2 will take you straight to the Minnesota Gopher.

If you want to try out Blue Skies, you can look for the software on the
Gopher, **downwind.sprl.umich.edu**, in the Software menu. Currently, there
are only versions for Macintosh and Power Macintosh; however, a Windows
version is under development. There is also a Welcome to Blue-Skies! file in
that menu that tells you more about the Blue Skies software.

Fig. 15.4

A weather map displayed by Blue Skies can be used to see weather information interactively.

A final word

A Gopher server remains an easy way to organize and present information on the Internet. It sometimes may not be as elegant as the World Wide Web; however, its utility as a flexible workhorse of an Internet server is unmatched. The primary weaknesses of Gopher as a service are the overburdened Veronica and Archie servers. This is only a weakness because of these servers' popularity. With the expansion of the Internet, perhaps more of those servers can be provided as a public service by some of the corporate Internet users or provided by commercial Internet companies for their subscribers. Either way would relieve some of the traffic from the university and network organization sites that currently provide these search servers.

Gopher as an access method does have some limitations in its current form. As we have seen, however, those limitations can be overcome. The application of new ideas to this older Internet technology has resulted in some creative approaches to displaying Gopher resources. It may be that the future of Gopher will only be limited by the imagination of a new generation of programmers.

Part VII:

Appendixes

Other Gopher Software

Whatever Gopher software you use, the information you access from each server will always be the same. As long as the server is available across the Internet, it responds to any client that knocks on its door asking for a connection. Though the actual information from the server is the same, each Gopher client displays it in its own way.

There are a number of Gopher programs to choose from. Most of the applications mentioned in this book are available for free from the Internet itself. Because most are free, you can try several clients and choose the one you think is best.

Most of the Gopher clients discussed in this chapter were found at the University of Minnesota's Gopher software archive. To retrieve these files yourself, Gopher or FTP to **boombox.micro.umn.edu** and look in the gopher/Windows directory.

Hgopher

Hgopher is a freely available Windows Gopher client written by Martyn Hampson. It's available from many FTP sites. The main place to find the latest version is **lister.cc.ic.ac.uk** in the /pub/wingopher directory. The file name is hgopher2.3.zip.

Hgopher displays each Gopher directory in a window. The top item on each list takes you back to the previous window. Icons beside each item identify whether the particular item is a file, directory, or other resource.

The Hgopher interface is simple and provides easy navigation of the Internet. The first time you launch Hgopher, it opens a file that contains pointers to some Gopher locations, as figure A.1 shows. From there, it's click and go.

Fig. A.1
The Hgopher interface, including a link to a familiar sight, the Mother Gopher at the University of Minnesota.

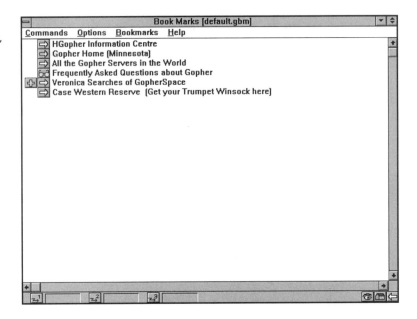

Installing Hgopher is very easy. Simply use a utility such as PKUNZIP to uncompress the hgopher2.3.zip file, create an icon in a Program Manager group by dragging the hgopher.exe file icon into the group where you want its icon to be, and you're done.

 Plain English, please!

Zip files are files that have been compressed with the shareware PKZIP.EXE. **Compressing** the files means they take less space to store, and most importantly, less time to download. To **decompress** zip files, or unzip them, you need a copy of the program PKUNZIP.EXE. Both files are available at FTP sites. **99**

The icons for each item in an Hgopher window have a couple of purposes. The icon on the far left tells you if there is any Gopher+ information about the item. The other icon tells you what type of Gopher item that line points to.

Q&A

I clicked on an Hgopher icon, but nothing happened. What's wrong?

You may be used to clicking an icon to make something happen. In Hgopher, though, you have to click on the item's descriptive text, not the icon. Double-clicking the text navigates to the new Gopher directory, or begins a file retrieval. Click the text and Hgopher leads you through Gopherspace.

The far left Hgopher icon, if it's there, tells you if a file has Gopher+ information available. Clicking on the icon shows the Gopher+ information for that item. It may be available in multiple formats. A text file might be stored in both plain text and Microsoft Word format. Or there could be versions of the file in different languages—French and English, for example.

 Plain English, please!

Gopher+ is a protocol which was developed several years ago to allow Gopher to provide access to non-text information types. Graphics, sound files, and other data types can be accessed effectively using Gopher+. Not all servers are Gopher+ servers, nor will all clients make effective use of Gopher+ documents.

The center icons identify the types of files in the directory. An arrow pointing right means you can connect to another directory. A pair of glasses mean there's a text file for you to read. A camera indicates an image file.

 (Tip)

The Hgopher Help file has a page that lists each icon and the Gopher item that it represents. From the <u>H</u>elp menu, choose <u>S</u>earch, and search for *icon* to find the Help topic Gopher Symbols.

Hgopher lets you save favorite Gopher places and files into a bookmark. You can save separate bookmark files as well, and control which bookmark file Hgopher opens at startup. Perhaps most importantly, there's a help file that describes the features of Hgopher.

Even without delving into the help file for details, Hgopher is simple to install and an easy way to cruise Gopherspace.

Gopher for Windows

Gopher for Windows is a quick and lean Internet client from the Computing Services Center of The Chinese University of Hong Kong. Among other FTP sites, it can currently be found at **ftp.cyberspace.com** in the /pub/ppp/windows/gopher directory. The application looks very plain, but its connections are fast. There are no graphical icons, and few features are available from the pull-down menus.

To install Gopher for Windows:

1 Unzip the wgopher.zip file into its own directory.

2 Click on the wgopher.exe file and drag it into the Program Manager group of your choice.

Figure A.2 shows the Home Gopher that Gopher for Windows initially points to. Each new directory appears in a separate window. To show all the windows that are open, keep choosing Windows, Cascade from the menu bar.

Fig. A.2

The bare-bones interface of Gopher for Windows. It gets files fast, even if it doesn't look fancy. (The [D] to the left of the menu item stands for Document.)

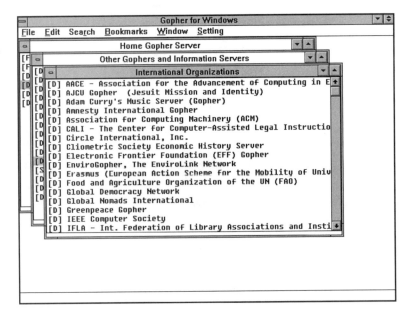

Gopher for Windows lets you save locations through bookmarks. You can define Telnet programs and image viewers as helper applications. Beyond that, however, this Gopher client is pretty much a point-and-shoot interface to Gopherspace.

Gopher Book

Gopher Book is an interesting experiment in software design, if nothing else. The program displays each Gopher menu as a page in a book. As you navigate Gopherspace, each new Gopher menu appears on its own page. You can even click on a bookmark in the book to display your Gopher bookmarks. Among other sites, you can currently get gophbook.zip at **boombox.micro.umn.edu** in the /pub/gopher/Windows/gophbook directory.

To install the Gopher Book:

1 Create a directory for the application (c:\gophbook. for example).

2 Copy the file (gophbook.zip) into that directory.

3 From DOS, uncompress the file with PKUNZIP, using the -d parameter. The command line should look like: PKUNZIP -d gophbook.zip.

4 Create an icon for the application in Program Manager.

Figure A.3 shows the cover of the book, just after the application has launched.

Double-click the book's cover and you begin to explore Gopherspace, as shown in figure A.4. The Gopher Book lets you set up helper applications for Telnet, text, and image files. You can set bookmarks to remember places you visited. However, this client does not offer the flexibility of some of the other clients. Gopher Book has a novel interface, but lacks much of the practical necessities needed to use Gopher most effectively.

Fig. A.3
Read any good Gopher
servers lately?

Fig. A.4
Gopher Book displays
each Gopher menu as
a book page, such as
this site at North
Carolina.

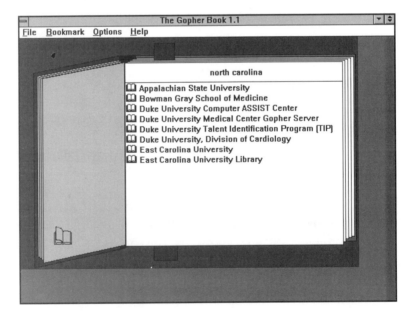

BCGopher

BCGopher was written by Edmund Greene at Boston College. This client lets you save bookmarks, and has a full selection of file types to configure for helper applications. You can change the font of the Gopher item descriptions as well.

Figure A.5 shows you what BCGopher looks like. Like Hgopher, BCGopher shows Gopher+ information with an icon to the left of the window. Click on the binoculars and BCGopher displays the Gopher+ information for that item. File types are indicated by the other icons. You can currently retrieve BCGopher from **ftp.ucdavis.edu** in the /win-public/Winsock/ directory.

Fig. A.5
BCGopher, a Gopher client from Boston College, uses different icons to represent various resources.

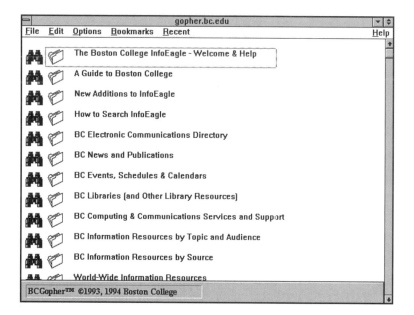

BCGopher installs from the file bcg08b.exe. Just copy the file to its own directory and double-click on it from the File Manager. When it's done, create an icon by clicking on the bcgopher.exe file and dragging it into a Program Manager group.

WinGopher

First released in the fall of 1993 by what was then NOTIS Systems, Inc., WinGopher was one of the first commercially available Windows Gopher clients. Originally written by Mark Gobat, WinGopher is now distributed as part of the WinPAC library searching tool from Ameritech Library Services. Figure A.6 shows WinGopher's interface.

Fig. A.6
WinGopher's friendly, easy-to-use interface identifies file and directory types by icons.

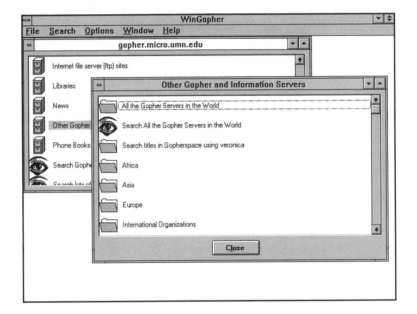

Like WSGopher, WinGopher is a full function program; each new Gopher directory displays in a new window. It uses icons to represent the different items encountered in Gopherspace: a file cabinet for a directory, a piece of paper for a text file. Its collections feature lets you organize the Gopher locations you want to visit again. You can currently retrieve WinGopher from **boombox.micro.umn.edu** in the /pub/gopher/Windows/WinGopher directory.

The Gopher software archive at the University of Minnesota has a text file that describes WinGopher and tells you who to contact to get the product. Because it's now sold with library searching software, you may come across this Gopher at your library.

NetManage Gopher

The NetManage Gopher comes with NetManage's Internet Chameleon products and is available as a commercial product only. It installs with the rest of the NetManage Internet software, like their FTP, Telnet, Mail and News programs. This Gopher has an interface that looks a lot like the Windows File Manager, as you can see from figure A.7.

To find out more, you can contact them at (408) 973-7171 or **sales@netmanage.com**.

Fig. A.7
If your Internet connection software is from NetManage, then you probably already have a copy of this Gopher program.

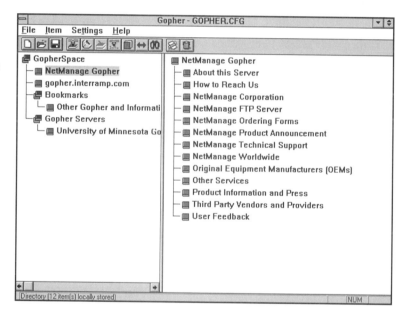

NetManage's Gopher has a toolbar for easy access to frequently used commands. The Preferences dialog box lets you configure a Telnet program and select a default download directory. It launches NotePad to view text files, and retrieves other types of files through a Save As dialog box.

Understanding Internet Connections

Before you get started searching Gopherspace, you need to get your PC connected to the Internet. The type of Gopher software you can use depends on the kind of Internet account you open. This appendix will help explain the two main types of Internet connections.

Getting to the Internet

Getting yourself on the Internet can seem like a daunting task. Sometimes it still seems like the best place for information about how to hook into the Net is on the Net itself. It's a catch-22. But don't despair; the situation is changing. Businesses are setting up shop for the sole reason to get YOU online. You're not alone anymore.

Getting a connection—where to look

There may not be a Yellow Pages section called "Internet Access Providers" yet, but look for it soon. To find out what companies provide access near you, check the following places:

- **Internet magazines**. These have ads for major national and international Internet providers.

- **Bookstores**. These carry directories of Internet providers.

- **Local newspaper stories** about the Internet. These may mention local access providers.

- **Anyone you know or meet** who is online. He may be able to recommend a provider.

Which ever way you choose to go, there are many companies waiting to hook you into the Net. Choose one, and ask for some trial time online so you can evaluate its service.

Regardless of where you find access, you'll probably be asked to make some choices. A shell account or a SLIP/PPP connection? Should you pay a flat monthly rate, or by the hour? There are as many different pricing schemes as there are providers. But the first question here—shell or SLIP/PPP?—should be easy to answer.

 Plain English, please!

A **shell account** allows you access to the Internet through an account on a host computer. From this account, you can run software on that host. **SLIP/PPP** are dial-up protocols that allow you to run Internet software directly from your PC. SLIP stands for Serial Line Interface Protocol and PPP for Point to Point Protocol. Many providers allow you to make use of SLIP/PPP connections to access the Internet.

Figure B.1 illustrates the difference between a shell account and a SLIP/PPP connection. The shell account connects you to a computer that is on the Internet. A SLIP/PPP connection hooks your PC into the Net.

Fig. B.1
The difference between a shell account and a SLIP/PPP connection is that SLIP/PPP accounts bring the Internet straight to your PC's desktop.

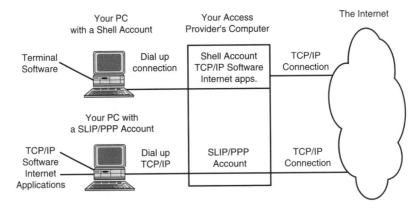

Shell accounts

A shell account is probably the most technically simple of the ways to connect to the Internet, and to Gopherspace. Basically, a shell account gives you the right to log into a computer that is on the Internet. You then navigate the Net as a terminal on that machine.

Do you prefer DOS to Windows? Would you rather use vi on a UNIX machine than the latest multimedia Macintosh? If you answered yes to either of these questions, then all you'll ever need is a shell account.

A shell account is usually the most inexpensive way to access the Internet, besides logging on for free through school or work. It's real Internet access, and you can use Gopher, read UseNet, and send e-mail; you can even browse the World Wide Web. But its limitations are important to understand.

- Access is through the remote host; your machine is not on the Internet. Files you retrieve are stored on the host and must be downloaded to your machine in a separate step.

- Clients are character based: no Windows interface, no immediate display of graphics or sound.

- You may be limited in the amount of disk space you are allowed on the host, or charged for storage space.

If you're using a personal computer that runs Windows, there's really no reason to limit your Internet experience to just a shell account. Step up to the next level: SLIP/PPP or a direct connection.

SLIP/PPP and direct connections

Other than shell accounts, the next level of Internet access lets you access the Net directly, either through a network or dial-up. If you're lucky, or rich, or can get online through work, you can get a direct network connection. Direct connections are the most expensive form of access, so they're not generally an option for most home users.

The route most people take is to open a SLIP/PPP account with an access provider. Again, the price of these accounts varies widely. Some companies charge a flat fee with unlimited time; others charge a lower monthly rate, but charge per hour after you've been online a certain amount of time.

Whether you're blessed with a direct connection or have a SLIP/PPP account, you need to run some communications software on your PC to complete the connection.

Remember in Chapter 1, "The Why, What, and Where of Gopher," where it said that the underlying language of the Internet was a protocol called TCP/IP? Well, to use SLIP/PPP, your PC must be able to talk TCP/IP with the Internet. The software programs that enable your PC to talk TCP/IP are called stacks.

From a user's point of view, the big difference between a SLIP/PPP dial-up connection and a direct network connection is the speed. Both types of connection require a TCP/IP stack, and each lets you use the same clients. There's just no way for a modem to send and receive data as fast as a direct network connection.

With either a SLIP/PPP or direct connection, and talking to TCP/IP with the Internet, you'll be able to choose Internet software. Remember, your access provider will probably provide you with some software. And after you're on the Net, there's plenty of software to be found.

How direct is direct?

A direct connection can be obtained in one of two ways. The first is by obtaining access on a network. The network generally makes use of a high bandwidth phone line connection (such as a T1, T3, or other leased line). Because these lines can contain much more information than a standard home phone line, many computers can send and receive information over them. Most computers access a network directly through the use of Ethernet or some other direct, non-modem method.

The second type of direct connection is through SLIP/PPP access. Basically, SLIP/PPP are protocols that allow you to pretend you are a network while you're using a phone line. You usually obtain a temporary Internet Protocol (IP) address while connected. This allows you to travel all over the Internet just as if you were on a network, but at a much slower rate!

SLIP/PPP—easy as 1-2-3

Confused? Don't be discouraged by the acronyms. Connecting to the Internet with a SLIP/PPP account requires three things:

- **An account and modem**—Your connection to the Internet through an Internet Access Provider.

- **A TCP/IP stack**—The software that lets your PC talk TCP/IP, like Trumpet Winsock or the Internet Sampler from NetManage. Some operating systems, such as Windows NT 3.5x and OS/2 Warp come with TCP/IP capabilities built-in.

- **Internet clients**—The software you really want to use to send mail, read news, and explore Gopherspace.

Remember, the access providers are in the business of getting you online. Most of them will help you get the software you need, and get it set up. Some even preconfigure the software so all you need to do is install it. When you're shopping providers, ask about the software and assistance they provide and how easy it is to set up a connection.

Part VIII:

Indexes

Action Index

General questions

When you need to...	You'll find help here
Understand Gopher and the Net	pp. 19–24
Gopher from AOL, CompuServe, or other services	pp. 191–203
Gopher from the World Wide Web	pp. 205–213
Choose a Gopher program	pp. 30–31 and 263–271

Getting started

When you need to...	You'll find help here
Get a copy of WSGopher	pp. 31–35
Install WSGopher	pp. 36–38
Get connected to the Internet	pp. 273–276
Gopher by address	pp. 59–61
Know what the directory icons mean	pp. 48–51
Know what the toolbar buttons mean	pp. 47–48
Know what you can find with Gopher	pp. 15–17
Find status information	pp. 48–51
Know where to start Gophering	pp. 61–64

Learning your way around

When you need to...	You'll find help here
Know why WSGopher didn't connect	pp. 43-45
Get back to your Home Gopher	p. 69
Change your Home Gopher	pp. 69-70
Move bookmarks to different categories	pp. 87-88
Rename a category	p. 85
Organize your bookmarks	pp. 83-89
Retrieve a file	pp. 70-73
See a sample Gopher search	p. 52 and pp. 55-56
Delete Gopher files from your PC	pp. 113-115
Send a bookmark to someone	pp. 89-91

Using bookmarks

When you need to...	You'll find help here
Save the place of something so you can return to it	pp. 80-82
Create a new bookmark category	pp. 84-85
Create your custom view of the Internet	p. 91
Delete a bookmark	pp. 85-86
Edit a bookmark	pp. 88-89
Fetch a bookmark	pp. 77-79
Get back to a place you saved	pp. 77-79

Viewers and Telnet programs

When you need to...	You'll find help here
Set up helper applications	pp. 95–102
Display a file after it downloads	pp. 72–73
Find help for Gopher	pp. 103–104
Know why Gopher needs help	p. 94
Define a Telnet program	pp. 101–103
Define viewers in File Manager	pp. 96–98
Define viewers in WSGopher	pp. 98–101

Saving, printing, copying, and so on

When you need to...	You'll find help here
Save a file after WSGopher quits	pp. 72–73
Save a text file	pp. 110–111
Save other kinds of Gopher files	pp. 111–113
Define directories where files get saved	pp. 108–109
Print a file or directory	pp. 114–117
See what a page looks like before printing it	pp. 115–116
Change the fonts WSGopher uses	pp. 119–121
Choose a default category	p. 83
Copy things to the Clipboard	p. 118

Searching in Gopherspace

When you need to...	You'll find help here
Search with Jughead	pp. 129-134
Find Jughead searches	pp. 127-128
Get online help from Jughead	pp. 134-135
Search with Veronica	pp. 139-144
Find specific file types with Veronica	pp. 146-147
Find a good Veronica server	pp. 149-156
Access a Veronica server directly	pp. 154-156
Know the difference between Jughead and Veronica	pp. 138-139
See the kinds of Archie searches you can do	pp. 161-168
Do an Archie search from Gopher	pp. 167-168
Do an Archie search via a Telnet session	pp. 168-173
Search a WAIS database	pp. 178-182
Know how WAIS is different from Veronica, Jughead, and Archie	p. 176
Find WAIS databases	pp. 178-182

Index

Symbols

* (asterisk) wildcard, 132-133
   in Veronica searches, 143

A

AARNET (Australia) server, 154
Academic Physician and Scientist site (academic medicine positions), 239
Academic Positions Network site (academic positions), 238
accessing
   Archie, 160-161
   Internet information, 10-14
   UseNet through universities, 22
   Veronica servers, 154-156
accounts, 277
   shell accounts, connecting to Internet with, 274-275
   SLIP/PPP, 274
     clients, 277
     connecting to Internet with, 275-276
     TCP/IP stack, 277
Add Bookmark command (Bookmark menu), 81

Add Directory Bookmark command (Bookmark menu), 83
adding bookmarks
   for directories, 82-83
   for one item, 80-82
   to default category, 83
addresses
   Brooks, Dave (WSGopher developer), 30
   browsers
     Enhanced Mosaic, 210
     NCSA Mosaic, 211
     Netscape Navigator, 212
   connecting to sites with, 59-61
   FTP archives, 104
   Gopher sites, searching for, 69-70
   in URLs (Uniform Resource Locators), 208
   Jughead, All Known Jughead Servers list, 128
   saving, *see* bookmarks
   Veronica servers, list of, 154-156
   WinGopher, 270
   see also URLs (Uniform Resource Locators); sites
advertisement sites, 240
?all command (Jughead searches), 134-135

All Known Jughead servers list
   address, 128
All the Gopher Servers in the World directory
   connecting to, 66
   retrieving, 64-66
America Online, 192-196
   Veronica searches, 155
American Heart Association site, 220
AND (logical operator), 147-150
anonymous FTP (File Transfer Protocol), 32, 160
   searching archives with, *see* Archie
ANU (Australian National University) database, 180
AOL, *see* America Online
APN (Academic Positions Network) site, 238
applications, *see* helper applications
Archie, 159-161
   accessing, 160-161
   exact searches, 161-164
   reading results of search, 171
   regular expression searches, 162, 166-167
   retrieving FTP files via Gopher to FTP gateway, 172-173

X-Y-Z